EASY-TO-MAKE
DOUGHNUTS

EASY-TO-MAKE
DOUGHNUTS

50 delectable recipes for plain,
glazed, sugar-dusted and filled delights,
in 200 step-by-step photographs

Written and photographed by
MOWIE KAY

aquamarine

Contents

Delightful doughnuts

Light, fluffy, sweet and moreish, deep-fried dough is the ultimate sweet treat, and variations of doughnuts are found in many forms throughout the world. Whether dusted with sugar, oozing with jam or glazed with chocolate, today doughnuts are undeniable crowd-pleasers, appearing everywhere from the stalls of street vendors to family bakeries and high-class restaurants.

Doughnuts, despite their contemporary popularity, are not a new invention. Countries all around the globe have age-old recipes for fried batters and doughs, which tend to be coated or filled with something sweet. Doughnuts are believed to have originated from Holland, and the original doughnut is thought to be the Dutch Oliebollen, which are little round balls of dough fried in oil and coated in sugar. These are understood to have been brought over to America by the Dutch, and evolved into what we now know as doughnuts.

DOUGHNUT VARIETIES

I have incorporated a broad range of doughnut types into this book, from traditional yeast-risen recipes to modern baked varieties. Doughnuts come in many shapes and sizes. The traditional shape is a ring with the hole in the middle – like the irresistible version bought at the seaside and fairgrounds, warm from the fryer and coated in sugar. I have fond memories of competing with friends to see who can resist licking the

Doughnut holes were originally made from the dough cut from the middle of a doughnut ring.

The same dough recipe can be shaped, coated, topped or filled to make many different doughnuts.

sugar from their lips the longest! For filled doughnuts, the dough is rolled into a ball, which is then hollowed slightly with the handle of a spoon, for filling. However, around the world, doughnuts also come in pillows, triangles, squares, sticks and practically any other shape possible. You can use cookie cutters to cut the dough into interesting shapes and sizes. I have stuck to traditional shapes in this book, but feel free to experiment – the doughnut dough is very versatile.

HOW TO USE THIS BOOK

Over the next few pages, I will guide you through the process of making doughnuts, from the equipment you will need to useful tips I have learned along the way. There follows 50 different doughnuts to make. Each doughnut recipe is very versatile and can be altered according to your individual taste. Each recipe is 'complete', so you can follow it from start to

Doughnuts can be presented very elegantly, and are an unusual addition to an afternoon tea selection.

Use a tiny dab of food colouring paste to create delectable pastel glazes, or opt for indulgent chocolate toppings.

finish, with handy technique photographs of tricky stages. However, once you have got the hang of making them, you can flick through the pages and 'mix and match' between recipes, which will give you endless combinations. For example, try the gluten-free doughnut with the chocolate fudge glaze, or take the topping from a fried doughnut and use it in a baked doughnut instead.

The first chapter covers the classics, and is a good place to start. Once you have mastered the basic sugar-dusted ring, you will find it simple to progress to more complex filled and topped recipes. The second chapter covers traditional world recipes, from Spanish churros with chocolate dipping sauce to South African Koeksisters. In the final chapter, I brought together some of my favourite flavour combinations that take inspiration from cuisines and ingredients from around the world.

Doughnuts everywhere

There are almost as many doughnuts in the world as there are countries, and I have tried to include some of the most popular ones in this book, as well as some of the deliciously unusual recipes. Some of the offerings may not look as we expect a doughnut to look; they come in such a fabulous array of sizes, moulded and twisted into a variety of shapes. In essence, however, they all follow similar recipes and the same principle of deep-frying a sweet dough until fluffy and crisp. Perfection!

FESTIVE BITES

Like many other delicious sweet bites, doughnuts are made and eaten around the world during times of celebration. Traditional Dutch Oliebollen, often referred to as the original doughnut, are usually made and enjoyed around New Year, specifically on New Years Eve to bring in the New Year. They are also eaten at funfairs, similar to the German Berliner (also known as the Berliner Pfannkuchen). The Berliner is

Oliebollen are removed from the hot oil by a Dutch baker.

a traditional German classic made from yeast dough, which is fried in oil and filled with jam. The Berliner is also enjoyed during the celebratory German Carnival days.

This is seen all around the world, for various festivals and celebrations. It is incredible that such a basic concept, dough fried in oil, can have so many different variations: Greek Loukoumades are dipped in sugar syrup and can be sprinkled with pistachios; Spanish Churros are piped directly into hot oil and later dipped into a rich chocolate sauce; South African

Koeksisters are braided and dipped in ice cold syrup, which gives them a crunchy outer covering.

THE HYBRID CRAZE

Today there are endless possibilities when it comes to making doughnuts. Creative contemporary bakers have developed new ideas that take the essence of the doughnut and turn it into something new and exciting. By combining a doughnut with a croissant, a new baking craze has been invented, which has swept the globe – croissant-style dough is

Doughnut-croissant hybrids became popular in American bakeries, and are now eaten worldwide.

shaped into a doughnut and deep-fried to create a delicious, buttery and crisp mouthful.

Another popular combination is a fusion of muffin and doughnut: a cakey doughnut with a jam filling and sugar-coated surface. The popularity of this produce is a reflection of the recent interest in cake doughnuts, and there are a few baked recipes to try in this book. I hope you enjoy them!

Loukoumades are soaked in a sumptuous sugar syrup before being served at a Greek festival.

Freshly fried churros are served all over Spain, dusted in icing sugar and cinnamon.

Basic ingredients

The best part about making doughnuts is that you only need very basic ingredients for a plain variety, most of which can probably already be found in your storecupboard. I recommend using the best-quality ingredients you can afford, as you will certainly notice the difference in the eating.

FLOUR

The best flour to use for a yeast-based doughnut is a strong white bread flour. This gives the doughnut a lighter, fluffier texture. You can also use plain (all-purpose) flour, but this turns out slightly chewier and not quite as soft. For baked doughnuts, however, plain flour is the best option. You can also mix it up by substituting half the flour for wholemeal (whole-wheat) flour, or try rice flour or gluten-free flour for interesting textures.

YEAST

The main ingredient for making your doughnuts light and fluffy, I have used easy-blend (rapid-rise) dried yeast for many recipes in this book, which is available in sachets. Yeast is sensitive to temperature, so it is important to use lukewarm milk in the dough, as the temperature activates the yeast, which in turn produces gases that aerate the

Wholemeal flour.

dough. If the milk is cold, it will still activate the yeast, just not as quickly, so you may need to increase the proving time. If the milk is hot, it can kill the yeast, rendering it ineffective.

Easy-blend dried yeast.

BAKING POWDER

An alternative raising agent to yeast, baking powder gives a light dough. The result is quite different to yeast as baking powder tends to make the dough more cake-like, as opposed to the velvety bread-like texture you get from yeast dough.

EGGS

The eggs used in this book are all medium (US large). I tend to use free-range organic eggs, as they provide superior flavour. Be sure to use the freshest eggs possible for the best results.

BUTTER

A small amount of butter is used in the dough; it helps bring the dough together and gives a velvety texture to the finished product. For yeast doughs, it is best to use chilled butter.

Eggs.

Butter.

Low-sodium salt flakes.

Caster sugar.

Sunflower oil.

SALT

Use salt very sparingly in most doughnut doughs – usually just a pinch is needed to heighten the flavours of all the other ingredients. If you can taste the salt in the finished product, you may have used too much, but if you don't use any at all, the dough will end up tasting quite bland. If you choose to eliminate the salt altogether, reduce the proving time of a yeast dough, as salt acts as a regulator for the yeast, reducing the speed it works. For salted caramel doughnuts, which are topped with salt flakes, I use low-sodium salt flakes, to reduce the amount of sodium in the recipe overall.

SUGAR

Used to encourage the yeast and sweeten the dough, caster (superfine) sugar is best for use in doughnut mixtures. It is also used for sprinkling over the doughnuts once they are baked. Typically, caster sugar would be sprinkled over, but there are a variety of other sugars to choose from for dusting, including soft and powdery icing (confectioners') sugar, and crunchy demerara (raw) sugar, as well as flavoured or spiced sugars. Icing sugar is mixed with liquid to create various glazes for coating the doughnuts. Just add water to icing sugar and stir until smooth

MILK

Use lukewarm milk in your dough, rather than straight from the refrigerator, as this will help the yeast to work at the right speed. Opt for full-fat (whole) milk for the best results.

OIL

The oil I have used to fry my doughnuts in this book is sunflower oil, but almost any vegetable oil can be used, as long as it does not have a strong flavour or a low smoke-point. You will need about 1 litre/1¾ pints/4 cups of oil, but this depends on the size of your pan. You can use a deep-fryer, which will give you more control over the temperature.

INSTANT FILLINGS

Try these simple and fast ideas for straight-from-the-cupboard doughnut fillings:

- jams and jellies
- nut butters
- ready-made chilled custard
- chocolate and hazelnut spread
- dulce de leche or caramel
- lemon or lime curd

Raspberry jam and peanut butter.

Dulce de leche.

Equipment for success

One of the great joys of making doughnuts is that you do not need any specialized equipment to achieve professional-looking results. There are certainly some electric appliances that will make the process easier, but they are by no means necessary. With a few basic tools, you will be whipping up doughnuts in no time.

STAND MIXERS

A handy appliance for making cakes and breads, a stand mixer is a useful but expensive tool. You can use a mixer to whip up doughnuts, if you like. It can be useful to have the mixer kneading the dough while you make the glaze or filling. However, I made the recipes in this book by hand, as I find kneading by hand results in a more elastic dough. Additionally, once you get the hang of it, using your hands is the best way of telling if the dough is ready.

DOUGHNUT CUTTERS

Special doughnut cutters are available to purchase online and at specialist baking stores. These form a ring-shape with the hole in the middle. Any other cookie cutter can also be used to create interesting shaped doughnuts, just bear in mind that the dough rises and expands while proving and frying, so cutters with sharp edges like stars do not work very well. If you cannot get your hands on a doughnut cutter, simply use a round cookie cutter to cut circles in the rolled out dough, then use the round part of a piping nozzle to cut out the hole in the centre.

BAKING PARCHMENT

Once I have shaped the doughnuts, I leave them to prove on small squares of baking parchment. Having the doughnuts on individual pieces of paper makes it easier to transfer them to the hot oil, without distorting their shape. Gently lift the corners of the baking paper, and transfer the doughnut gently into the hot oil. If the dough does not slide off easily, just place it in the oil all together, paper-side up. The paper comes off quickly and you can then use tongs or a slotted spoon to lift the paper out of the oil while the doughnuts fry.

CLEAR FILM (PLASTIC WRAP)

Use clear film to cover the dough after kneading it, to keep the moisture in the dough and prevent the dough from drying out. If the dough dries out, it forms a skin on the surface and forms hard areas in the cooked doughnuts. If you do not have any clear film, use a dampened dish cloth.

PAN

I like to use a pan for frying doughnuts. It is important to use a heavy deep pan for frying in oil. The deeper the pan, the less likely you are to get any splashes. Try to avoid using non-stick pans for deep-frying, as high temperatures can reduce the non-stick properties.

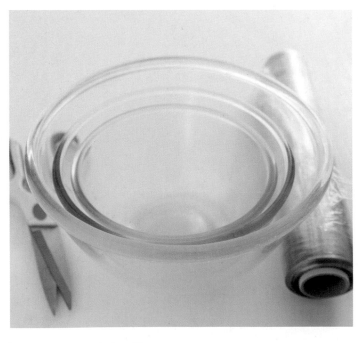

Mixing bowls and clear film.

Various doughnut cutters.

Sugar thermometer.

Kitchen towels and slotted spoon.

Doughnut baking trays.

SUGAR THERMOMETER

This is an important tool for checking the temperature of the frying oil when using a pan. The oil should be around 170°C/340°F. If you do not have a sugar thermometer, you can test to see if the oil is hot enough by placing a small piece of bread into the oil. If it bubbles and turns a golden brown within 30 seconds, then the oil is hot enough to fry doughnuts in. If it browns more quickly than that, it is too hot; if it does not brown in that time, it is too cool.

DEEP-FRYER

Although I use a pan for deep-frying in the recipes, you can use a deep-fryer, if you have one. These can be useful, especially for keeping the oil temperature constant, which ensures even cooking. The main body is filled with oil, the temperature is set and the doughnuts are placed into the oil. There is a basket nestling in most deep-fryers, with handles that can be used to lift the doughnuts out of the fryer.

SLOTTED SPOON

Use a long-handled slotted spoon to lift the cooked doughnuts out of the oil, keeping hands at a safe distance.

TONGS

These can be used alongside or instead of a slotted spoon; some people find tongs easier to work with. Use long-handled tongs to keep your hands away from the oil, but be gentle when lifting the doughnuts so that you do not distort their shapes.

KITCHEN PAPER

You will need plenty of absorbent kitchen paper on which to place the cooked doughnuts from the pan.

Piping bags and nozzles.

The paper will absorb the excess oil before you dust them with sugar or glaze them.

DOUGHNUT BAKING TRAY

These are usually shaped as rings, but they also come in novelty shapes, as well as mini doughnuts. These trays are perfect for my baked doughnuts, which have a sumptuous cakey texture.

ELECTRIC DOUGHNUT COOKER

These modern appliances are similar to a waffle-maker, and they produce perfect 'baked style' ring doughnuts with no oil. Yeast-based doughs are not suited to these doughnut cookers.

PIPING BAGS AND NOZZLES

Disposable piping (pastry) bags are inexpensive and save you washing reusable bags or making them from baking parchment. For filling doughnuts, just snip off the end; no nozzle is needed. Piping bags are also used for piping doughnut batters, such as for Churros or Crullers; use a star-shaped nozzle for these. I also pipe batter into doughnut baking tins – this allows for even distribution of dough, and makes the finished products much neater.

Simple techniques

Having baked thousands of doughnuts while writing this book, with stage after stage of testing and re-testing, I can now share with you some very handy tips. From the length of time to prove your dough and simple tricks for creating perfect rounds to safe frying advice and decorating techniques, all you need to know to create divine doughnuts is covered on the following pages.

The key to successful doughnut-making is preparation. I like to get all my ingredients and equipment ready (known as 'mise en place') before starting, so I can check I have got everything I need and prevent rushing around mid-recipe. Weigh out all your ingredients before you begin, and place them all in separate bowls nearby. Whether making a yeast-risen dough or a tray of baked bites, planning ahead is key.

MAKING YEAST DOUGH

The classic doughnut dough is made with yeast. It is similar to a bread dough and needs plenty of time to rise, so you should start making your dough about 2 hours before you want to fry the doughnuts. Sift the flour together with the yeast, sugar, salt and any other dry ingredients into a bowl. Add the chilled butter, and rub this in until the mixture looks crumbly. At this point, add the eggs and milk, and knead the dough

into a ball in the bowl. Sprinkle some flour on to a clean work surface and turn out the dough. The dough will be very sticky at this point. Knead the dough for 10 minutes by hand (or with the hook attachment on an electric mixer), until you have a light, elastic dough. Be patient – it will come together. Form the dough into a ball, place into a lightly oiled bowl and cover with clear film (plastic wrap) or a damp dish towel. Baking sprays are useful for oiling the bowl, as you only need a minimal amount.

PROVING YEAST DOUGH

The dough needs to rest for up to 1 hour, depending on the temperature of the room. This allows the activated yeast to work, filling the dough with tiny air bubbles and allowing it to rise. If you do not let the dough prove for

The dough will double in size during the first proving.

KNEADING

When you start kneading the dough, it will be very sticky, and you may think that it is too sticky to handle. The trick is to keep kneading – it will all come together after about 10 minutes. Try not to add more flour than stated in the recipe, as this will make the dough tough, rubbery and elastic. What you are aiming for is a light and fluffy dough that feels like it will almost stick to your hands at the end of the kneading time, but actually comes away nicely.

During the second proving, the doughnuts become bigger and rounder.

The best way is to hold the dough ball in two hands and continually pull and stretch from the top to the bottom, tucking any extra folds of dough underneath and pinching tightly. This leaves the doughnuts with smooth tops, and it allows them to rise evenly.

For ring doughnuts, roll the dough out to about 1cm/½in thick, and use a doughnut cutter to cut out ring shapes. You can use other shapes of cutter too, if you like. Whatever the shape of doughnut, you need to place them on individual squares of baking parchment for the second proving. The baking parchment helps you to transfer the dough to the frying oil without distorting its shape. If the doughnuts are all on one sheet, it is very difficult to get them all into the oil without squashing some or sticking them together.

long enough, the result is a thick, heavy dough that is tough when fried. The dough should double in size at this stage. The dough is then shaped as needed, either rolled into balls with your hands, or rolled out flat with a rolling pin and then cut into rings.

SHAPING YEAST DOUGH
One of the most basic shapes you can form with the dough is a ball. However, do not be tempted to simply roll the dough between your hands, as this leaves lines and marks, which will be noticeable in the finished product.

PROVING DOUGHNUTS AGAIN
Allow the doughnuts to prove on their baking parchment squares for 30 minutes. The dough will rise slightly during this time, but will not double in bulk. During this stage you will see your doughnuts taking shape. After 30 minutes, they are ready for frying.

Cutting the dough into quarters first will help to create even pieces.

Do not waste the 'holes' – roll them back up for one more doughnut.

Place the doughnuts on baking parchment squares to prove again.

DEEP-FRYING TIPS

- When frying in batches, and if sprinkling with sugar in between, try not to get any sugar on the utensils being used to fish out the doughnuts from the pot. This sugar will settle to the bottom of the pan and caramelize to a black crisp. Always use clean utensils.
- It is a good idea to keep a plate nearby lined with some kitchen paper to place the slotted spoon onto when not in use.
- Keep a big heatproof bowl quite close to the frying pan into which you can discard any baking paper squares immediately after transferring the doughnuts into the oil.
- Sugar thermometers come with a clip that suspends the thermometer in the oil, without it touching the sides. Keep an eye on the temperature as it can fluctuate, dipping slightly as soon as the doughnuts are added and rising sharply if they fry too much.

Slotted spoon and kitchen paper.

Sugar thermometer.

HOT OIL DANGERS

Frying in oil can be very dangerous, as spills and splashes can easily cause burns. Take your time, and make sure the pan is stable on the hob. Keep a large metal lid nearby at all times while frying – in the unlikely event of the oil catching fire, turn off the heat source, and cover the pot immediately with the metal lid (a glass lid could shatter), and this should starve any flames of oxygen. Do not try to move the pan, and never, under any circumstances, put water or any other liquid into the hot oil. Never leave a pan of deep-frying oil unattended.

could bubble over and is more likely to spill. Heat the oil to the correct temperature, then gently transfer the doughnuts into the hot oil from the baking parchment squares. Use a slotted spoon or tongs to remove the cooked doughnuts from the oil.

BAKING DOUGHNUTS

In recent times, baked doughnuts have become popular since they are a little healthier, not being deep-fried, but also because they are easier and quicker to make than fried doughnuts. I am a big fan of baked doughnuts, especially when time is short and there is not enough time to prove a yeast dough.

When making baked doughnuts, it is important to know your oven – learn where the hot spots are and whether it cooks evenly. If one side is hotter than the other, you should turn your doughnut trays around half way through baking. You can use an electric doughnut cooker for any of the baked doughnut recipes in this book – follow the manufacturer's instructions.

FRYING DOUGHNUTS

The perfect temperature in which to fry doughnuts is somewhere between 160ºC/325ºF and 180ºC/350ºF. If the oil temperature is too low, the dough absorbs too much oil and becomes soggy. If the temperature is too high, the doughnuts brown too quickly on the outside and remain uncooked inside. I find that 170ºC/340ºF is the perfect temperature, with the doughnuts being cooked for 1–2 minutes on each side.

Frying on the hob is simple, with just a pan needed. Half fill a deep, heavy pan with about 1 litre/1¾ pints/4 cups of oil, or enough to allow the doughnuts to float on the surface while frying and not touch the base of the pan. Never fill a pan more than half way with oil as this

The baking parchment helps you to transfer the dough to the frying oil without distorting its shape.

COATING AND GLAZING

Decorating doughnuts is probably the easiest part of the whole doughnut making process. For a simple finish, just roll them in sugar. Caster (superfine) sugar is the best for traditional tastes, but you can try any other type of sugar too. If you do not serve them immediately and the sugar starts to dissolve, give them a second coating in sugar before you serve them. You can also glaze them with a variety of things, from simple coatings to extravagant toppings.

Wait until the doughnuts have cooled slightly before decorating, but are still warm. If the doughnuts are too warm when you decorate them with something like sugar, the warmth will cause the sugar to melt and this can end up looking clumpy. The same is true for a glaze; if the doughnuts are too warm, the glaze will absorb the heat and melt, and not set properly. This can result in cracks and very thin glazes.

When covering doughnuts in a glaze, spoon the glaze over the doughnuts, to give nice drizzles down the sides. Alternatively, dip the top side of the doughnut in the glaze, then lift it up, keeping the doughnut upside-down, and allow the excess glaze to drip off. This results in a clean circle of glaze just around the top that will not drizzle down.

MAKING A SIMPLE GLAZE

To make a glaze, mix some icing (confectioners') sugar with water until smooth. You can add more water for a thinner glaze, or more sugar for a thicker covering. You can flavour it with vanilla extract, lemon rind, fruit essences and similar.

GLAZING DOUGHNUTS

Spooning a thick glaze over the tops of the doughnuts will give an attractive finish as it drizzles down the sides.

A runny glaze can be used to coat the entire doughnut. Dip the doughnut into the glaze, while still slightly warm, to coat it all over. Place it on to a wire rack to set, with a piece of baking parchment underneath to catch any drips.

Simple sugar-dusted doughnuts are the perfect mid-morning treat.

FILLING

Adding filling to doughnuts is a simple process. Do not over-fill doughnuts, as this can make them too sweet and messy to eat. It is best to make the hole in the doughnut while it is still slightly warm. You can fill the doughnuts before icing, sprinkling or covering with a glaze, or the other way around. If you fill them first, the advantage is that you can handle the doughnuts from all sides without ruining the outside decoration or getting your hands full of sugar. If you are using a filling that requires chilling, you should fill the doughnuts only when you are about to serve. If you wish to fill them in advance, store the doughnuts in the refrigerator until you are ready to serve.

FILLING DOUGHNUTS

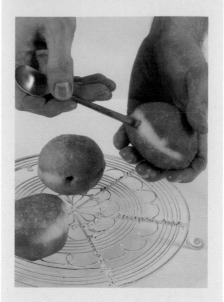

1 *Poke the handle of a teaspoon into the doughnut, and move it around in a circular motion to make a 'pocket' for the filling.*

2 *Fill a disposable piping (pastry) bag with the filling, snip off the end, and insert the tip of the piping bag into the hole. Squeeze a small amount of filling into each of the doughnuts.*

The classic filled doughnut contains a sweet jam centre and is dusted with caster sugar.

If freezing doughnuts, do so before adding any filling.

STORAGE

Most fried doughnuts are best eaten while still slightly warm, straight out of the fryer, filled or unfilled, and coated or glazed. This is when they are at their best – light, fluffy, pillowy, warm and chewy. However, there are a couple of doughnuts which benefit from being refrigerated for a few hours, or even overnight, such as the custard-filled doughnut, which sets firm, and the chocolate doughnut, which develops the consistency of chocolate cake. If you use any filling that needs to be chilled, such as cream or custard, you need to refrigerate the filled doughnuts, if you are not eating them straight away. They do not usually last that long in my house!

Baked doughnuts last slightly longer, similar to cakes. You can safely make these ahead of time, which is especially good news for the giant doughnut cake – perfect for birthdays! Store in an air-tight container for 1–2 days.

Cake doughnuts stay fresh longer than fried doughnuts, so they can be made a little in advance, if needed for a party or special occasion.

FREEZING DOUGHNUTS

If you are freezing doughnuts, do so as soon as they have cooled, tightly sealed in an airtight container. They must be frozen plain, without any sugar coating or filling as, when defrosting, the sugar melts on to the doughnut, resulting in a soggy dough. It is important to defrost them while they are still tightly sealed in their container, as this locks in the moisture. If doughnuts are defrosted on a wire rack, the condensation evaporates very quickly and, in so doing, draws out any moisture in the doughnuts and renders them dry. Once the doughnuts have completely defrosted, sprinkle with sugar or top with a glaze, and fill with your choice of filling, if needed. Eat within 24 hours, once defrosted.

CLASSIC DOUGHNUTS

This selection of doughnuts covers all the favourites, from traditional seaside sugary treats to contemporary confections found in city bakery window displays. Whether filled or ring-shaped, there is something here to tempt everyone – sticky caramel, indulgent chocolate, creamy custard or zesty lemon.

Simple sugar-dusted ring doughnuts

In my opinion, these are the ultimate classic doughnuts – light, fluffy, delicious and sweet. Once out of the oil, toss them in lots of sugar to coat, then tuck in while still warm. A batch of these traditional treats never lasts long. Try to resist licking the sugar off your lips after the first bite, if you can!

Makes | 12

225g/8oz/2 cups strong white bread flour, plus extra for dusting
7g/¼oz/1½ tsp easy-blend (rapid-rise) dried yeast
15ml/1 tbsp caster (superfine) sugar
a pinch of salt
65g/2½oz/5 tbsp butter, cubed and chilled
1 egg, beaten
120ml/4fl oz/½ cup full-fat (whole) milk, lukewarm
about 1 litre/1¾ pints/4 cups sunflower oil, for frying

For coating
115g/4oz/generous ½ cup caster (superfine) sugar

12 small squares of baking parchment

1 Sift the flour together with the yeast, sugar and salt into a bowl. Add the butter and rub into the flour mixture using your fingertips. Add the egg and milk, and knead the mixture until it all comes together.

2 Turn out the dough on to a lightly floured work surface and knead for 10 minutes, or until silky smooth. Roll into a ball and place in a clean, lightly greased bowl. Cover with clear film (plastic wrap) and leave to rest in a warm place for about 1 hour, or until doubled in size.

3 Roll out the dough on a lightly floured work surface until it is roughly 1cm/½in thick. Using a doughnut cookie cutter, cut out 12 rings and place each of these on to a baking parchment square. Cover loosely with clear film and leave to stand in a warm place for 30 minutes, until slightly risen.

4 Heat the oil for deep-frying in a large, deep pan to 170ºC/340ºF.

5 Gently lift the doughnuts using the edges of the baking parchment, without disturbing the doughnuts, and slide each one (minus the baking parchment) into the hot oil in batches of 3. Cook them for 30–60 seconds on each side, or until golden brown all over. Remove the doughnuts from the oil with a slotted spoon, and drain on kitchen paper.

6 Place the sugar for sprinkling on a plate. While the doughnuts are still slightly warm, toss them in the sugar, coating them all over.

Energy 203kcal/853kJ; Protein 2.6g; Carbohydrate 29.4g, of which sugars 16.3g; Fat 9.2g, of which saturates 2.4g; Cholesterol 10mg; Calcium 34mg; Fibre 0g; Sodium 95mg.

Plain glazed ring doughnuts

This recipe is for traditional glazed doughnuts. These are made with a classic yeast-raised dough, just like the sugar-dusted ones, but are coated with a simple and sweet glaze instead.

Makes |12

225g/8oz/2 cups strong white bread flour, plus extra for dusting
7g/¼oz/1½ tsp easy-blend (rapid-rise) dried yeast
15ml/1 tbsp caster (superfine) sugar
a pinch of salt
65g/2½oz/5 tbsp butter, cubed and chilled
1 egg, beaten
120ml/4fl oz/½ cup full-fat (whole) milk, lukewarm
about 1 litre/1¾ pints/4 cups sunflower oil, for frying

For the glaze
300g/11oz/2¾ cups icing (confectioners') sugar
50ml/2fl oz/¼ cup water

12 small squares of baking parchment

1 Sift the flour together with the yeast, sugar and salt into a bowl. Add the butter and rub into the flour mixture using your fingertips. Add the egg and milk, and knead the mixture until it all comes together.

2 Turn out the dough on to a lightly floured work surface and knead for 10 minutes or until silky smooth. Roll into a ball and place in a clean, lightly greased bowl. Cover with clear film (plastic wrap) and leave to rest in a warm place for about 1 hour, or until doubled in size.

3 Roll out the dough on a lightly floured work surface until it is roughly 1cm/½in thick. Using a doughnut cookie cutter, cut out 12 rings and place each of these on to a baking parchment square. Cover loosely with clear film and leave to stand in a warm place for 30 minutes, until slightly risen.

4 Heat the oil for deep-frying in a large, deep pan to 170°C/340°F.

5 Gently lift the doughnuts using the edges of the baking parchment, without disturbing the doughnuts, and slide each one (minus the baking parchment) into the hot oil in batches of 3. Cook them for 30–60 seconds on each side or until golden brown all over. Remove the doughnuts from the oil with a slotted spoon, and drain on kitchen paper.

6 Make the glaze by mixing the icing sugar and water together. Dip the doughnuts into the glaze. Allow to set.

Energy 264kcal/1112kJ; Protein 2.5g; Carbohydrate 45.6g, of which sugars 32.2g; Fat 9.2g, of which saturates 2.4g; Cholesterol 10mg; Calcium 32mg; Fibre 0g; Sodium 97mg.

Baked plain ring doughnuts

Here is a basic recipe for baked sugar-dusted doughnuts. This is a very versatile batter and results in perfect ring doughnuts when baked in a doughnut baking tin (pan). Vary the flavours by adding ground spices such as ginger or cinnamon to the batter, and try any of the glazes or toppings from the rest of this book, if you like.

Makes | 12

non-stick baking oil or melted butter,
 for greasing
100g/3¾oz/scant ½ cup
 butter, softened
150g/5oz/¾ cup caster
 (superfine) sugar
5ml/1 tsp vanilla extract
2 eggs
275g/10oz/2½ cups plain
 (all-purpose) flour
10ml/2 tsp baking powder
a pinch of salt
150ml/¼ pint/⅔ cup full-fat
 (whole) milk

For coating
115g/4oz/generous ½ cup caster
 (superfine) sugar

1 Preheat the oven to 180ºC/350ºF/ Gas 4. Spray a 12-cup doughnut baking tin (pan) or 2 6-cup doughnut baking tins with non-stick baking oil, or brush with melted butter.

2 Place the softened butter, sugar and vanilla extract in a bowl and whisk together until light and creamy. Add one egg at a time, whisking to make sure the first one is fully incorporated before adding the second.

3 Sift the flour, baking powder and salt into the mixture and fold in. Add the milk and mix just until it all comes together.

4 Transfer the mixture to a piping (pastry) bag fitted with a round nozzle, then pipe the mixture into the prepared baking tin, dividing it evenly between the cups. Piping the mixture makes it easier to create neat circles, but you can spoon the mixture into the tin, if you prefer.

5 Place the tin in the middle of the oven and bake for 15 minutes, or until golden brown. Remove from the oven and leave to stand for 5 minutes before removing the doughnuts from the tin.

6 Place the sugar for sprinkling on a plate. While the doughnuts are still slightly warm, toss them in the sugar, coating them all over.

Energy 251kcal/1055kJ; Protein 4g; Carbohydrate 41.5g, of which sugars 24g; Fat 8.8g, of which saturates 5g; Cholesterol 58mg; Calcium 60mg; Fibre 1g; Sodium 72mg.

Jam-filled doughnuts

These classic doughnuts are soft and pillowy and they are best eaten while still slightly warm, just after they've been filled with jam and dusted with sugar. I like the simple traditional taste of these, but to ring the changes, you can try adding 5ml/1 tsp ground cinnamon or other ground spices to the sugar before sprinkling.

Makes | 12

225g/8oz/2 cups strong white bread
  flour, plus extra for dusting
7g/¼oz/1½ tsp easy-blend
  (rapid-rise) dried yeast
15ml/1 tbsp caster (superfine) sugar
a pinch of salt
65g/2½oz/5 tbsp butter, cubed
  and chilled
1 egg, beaten
120ml/4fl oz/½ cup full-fat (whole)
  milk, lukewarm
about 1 litre/1¾ pints/4 cups
  sunflower oil, for frying

For the filling
60ml/4 tbsp raspberry jam

For coating
115g/4oz/generous ½ cup caster
  (superfine) sugar

12 small squares of baking
  parchment

1 Sift the flour together with the yeast, sugar and salt into a bowl. Add the butter and rub into the flour mixture using your fingertips. Add the egg and milk, and knead the mixture until it all comes together.

2 Turn out the dough on to a lightly floured work surface and knead for 10 minutes, or until silky smooth. Roll into a ball and place in a clean, lightly greased bowl. Cover with clear film (plastic wrap) and leave to rest in a warm place for about 1 hour, or until doubled in size.

3 Cut the dough into 12 even pieces, and roll the pieces into smooth round balls. Place each one on to a baking parchment square. Cover loosely with clear film and leave to stand in a warm place for 30 minutes, until slightly risen.

4 Heat the oil for deep-frying in a large, deep pan to 170°C/340°F.

5 Gently lift the doughnuts using the edges of the baking parchment, without disturbing the doughnuts, and slide each one (minus the baking parchment) into the hot oil in batches of 3. Cook them for 30–60 seconds on each side, or until golden brown all over. Remove the doughnuts from the oil with a slotted spoon, and drain on kitchen paper.

6 While the doughnuts are still warm, poke the handle of a teaspoon into the side of each doughnut, moving the handle around inside the doughnut in a circular motion to make room for the filling.

7 Fill a piping (pastry) bag with the jam and squeeze a small amount into each doughnut. Sprinkle the doughnuts with sugar on all sides, to coat them completely. Alternatively, place the sugar on a plate and toss the doughnuts in the sugar.

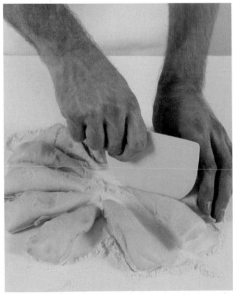

Energy 216kcal/909kJ; Protein 2.6g; Carbohydrate 32.8g, of which sugars 19.7g; Fat 9.2g, of which saturates 2.4g; Cholesterol 10mg; Calcium 35mg; Fibre 0g; Sodium 96mg.

Lemon doughnuts

Zesty and fresh, these doughnuts are made with lemon rind and filled with lemon curd for a glorious sweet-tart combination. The lemony dough is also nice filled with marmalade. You only need one lemon for this recipe – use half of the grated rind in the batter, and the other half for coating.

Makes | 12

225g/8oz/2 cups strong white bread flour, plus extra for dusting
7g/¼oz/1½ tsp easy-blend (rapid-rise) dried yeast
15ml/1 tbsp caster (superfine) sugar
a pinch of salt
finely grated rind of ½ lemon
65g/2½oz/5 tbsp butter, cubed and chilled
1 egg, beaten
120ml/4fl oz/½ cup full-fat (whole) milk, lukewarm
about 1 litre/1¾ pints/4 cups sunflower oil, for frying

For the filling
125g/4¼oz/scant ½ cup lemon curd

For coating
115g/4oz/generous ½ cup caster (superfine) sugar
finely grated rind of ½ lemon

12 small squares of baking parchment

1 Sift the flour together with the yeast, sugar and salt into a bowl. Add the lemon rind and butter, and rub into the flour mixture using your fingertips. Add the egg and milk, and knead the mixture until it all comes together.

2 Turn out the dough on to a lightly floured work surface and knead for 10 minutes, or until silky smooth.

3 Roll into a ball and place in a clean, lightly greased bowl. Cover with clear film (plastic wrap) and leave to rest in a warm place for about 1 hour, or until doubled in size.

4 Cut the dough into 12 even pieces, and roll into smooth round balls. Place each one on to a baking parchment square. Cover loosely with clear film and leave to stand in a warm place for 30 minutes, until slightly risen.

5 Heat the oil in a large, deep pan to 170°C/340°F.

6 Gently lift the doughnuts using the edges of the baking parchment, without disturbing the doughnuts, and slide each one (minus the baking parchment) into the hot oil in batches of 3. Cook them for 30–60 seconds on each side or until golden brown all over. Remove the doughnuts from the oil with a slotted spoon, and drain on kitchen paper.

7 While the doughnuts are still warm, poke the handle of a teaspoon into the side of each doughnut, moving the handle around inside the doughnut in a circular motion to make room for the filling.

8 Fill a piping (pastry) bag with the lemon curd and squeeze a small amount into each doughnut.

9 To coat the doughnuts, mix the caster sugar with the lemon rind, and spread out on a plate. Roll the doughnuts in the lemon sugar to coat them completely.

Energy 232kcal/978kJ; Protein 2.6g; Carbohydrate 35.9g, of which sugars 20.5g; Fat 9.7g, of which saturates 2.5g; Cholesterol 12mg; Calcium 35mg; Fibre 0g; Sodium 102mg.

Apple-cinnamon doughnuts

Apple and cinnamon is a classic combination that works beautifully with these doughnuts. I use whole slices of fresh eating apples, and envelop each slice in the delicate softness of delicious dough. Use a mandoline for slicing the apples into thin rings, to ensure they are thin enough to cook quickly.

Makes | 12

2 eating apples, cored
225g/8oz/2 cups strong white bread flour, plus extra for dusting
7g/¼oz/1½ tsp easy-blend (rapid-rise) dried yeast
15ml/1 tbsp caster (superfine) sugar
a pinch of salt
65g/2½oz/5 tbsp butter, cubed and chilled
1 egg, beaten
120ml/4fl oz/½ cup full-fat (whole) milk, lukewarm
about 1 litre/1¾ pints/4 cups sunflower oil, for frying

For coating
60ml/4 tbsp icing (confectioners') sugar
2.5ml/½ tsp ground cinnamon

12 small squares of baking parchment

1 Cut 6 3mm/⅛in rings from the middle section of each cored apple. Do not use the tops and bottoms, as the rings will be too small.

2 Sift the flour together with the yeast, sugar and salt into a bowl. Add the butter, and rub into the flour mixture using your fingertips. Add the egg and milk, and knead the mixture until it all comes together.

3 Turn out the dough on to a lightly floured work surface and knead for 10 minutes, or until silky smooth. Roll into a ball and place in a clean, lightly greased bowl. Cover with clear film (plastic wrap) and leave to rest in a warm place for about 1 hour, or until doubled in size.

4 Roll out the dough on a lightly floured work surface until it is roughly 5mm/¼in thick. Using a doughnut cookie cutter, cut out 24 rings.

5 Place 12 of the rings on to baking parchment squares and top each with a slice of apple. Cover with the remaining 12 dough rings and pinch the edges together to seal the apple slices inside. Cover loosely with clear film and leave to stand in a warm place for 30 minutes, until slightly risen.

6 Heat the oil in a large, deep pan to 170°C/340°F. Gently lift the doughnuts using the edges of the baking parchment, without disturbing the doughnuts, and slide each one (minus the baking parchment) into the hot oil in batches of 3. Cook them for 30–60 seconds on each side, or until golden brown all over. Remove the doughnuts with a slotted spoon, and drain on kitchen paper.

7 To coat the doughnuts, mix the icing sugar with the cinnamon, and, while the doughnuts are still slightly warm, toss them in the cinnamon sugar to coat completely.

  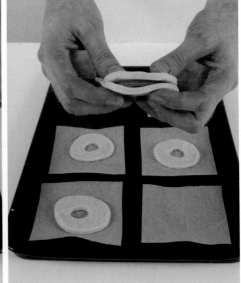

Energy 191kcal/801kJ; Protein 2.6g; Carbohydrate 26.1g, of which sugars 12.9g; Fat 9.2g, of which saturates 2.4g; Cholesterol 10mg; Calcium 34mg; Fibre 0.3g; Sodium 95mg.

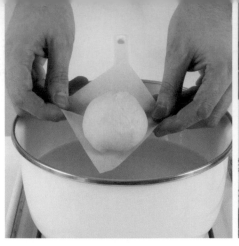 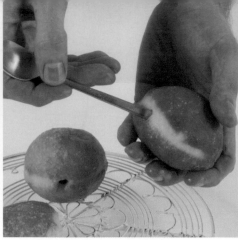 

Custard-filled doughnuts

A sumptuous custard filling transforms these doughnuts into something heavenly. If you are in a rush, you can use good quality ready-made cold custard. Pour any leftover custard into a small serving bowl and serve as a dipping sauce for extra custardy goodness. Refrigerate the doughnuts, if you are not serving them immediately.

Makes | 12

225g/8oz/2 cups strong white bread flour, plus extra for dusting
7g/¼oz/1½ tsp easy-blend (rapid-rise) dried yeast
15ml/1 tbsp caster (superfine) sugar
a pinch of salt
65g/2½oz/5 tbsp butter, cubed and chilled
1 egg, beaten
120ml/4fl oz/½ cup full-fat (whole) milk, lukewarm
about 1 litre/1¾ pints/4 cups sunflower oil, for frying

For the custard filling

250ml/8fl oz/1 cup full-fat (whole) milk
25ml/1½ tbsp single (light) cream
seeds from 1 vanilla pod (bean)
2 egg yolks
20g/¾oz/1½ tbsp caster (superfine) sugar
5ml/1 tsp cornflour (cornstarch)

For coating

115g/4oz/generous ½ cup caster (superfine) sugar

12 small squares of baking parchment

1 For the custard, place the milk, cream and vanilla seeds in a pan, and bring to a simmer over a low heat. In a bowl, whisk the egg yolks with the sugar and cornflour until combined. Pour the hot milk mixture into the egg mixture, stirring constantly. Pour the mixture back into the pan and cook over a low heat, stirring constantly, until smooth and thickened (do not allow the mixture to boil, or it may curdle). Remove from the heat.

2 Pour the custard into a heatproof bowl, cover the surface with clear film (plastic wrap) or baking parchment to prevent a skin forming, and leave to cool completely.

3 Meanwhile, sift the flour together with the yeast, sugar and salt into a bowl. Add the butter and rub into the flour mixture using your fingertips. Add the egg and milk, and knead the mixture until it all comes together.

4 Turn out the dough on to a lightly floured work surface and knead for 10 minutes, or until silky smooth. Roll into a ball and place in a clean, lightly greased bowl. Cover with clear film and leave to rest in a warm place for about 1 hour, or until doubled in size.

5 Cut the dough into 12 even pieces, and roll into smooth round balls. Place each one on to a baking parchment square. Cover loosely with clear film and leave to stand in a warm place for 30 minutes, until slightly risen.

6 Heat the oil in a large, deep pan to 170°C/340°F. Gently lift the doughnuts using the edges of the baking parchment, without disturbing the doughnuts, and slide each one (minus the baking parchment) into the hot oil in batches of 3. Cook them for 30–60 seconds on each side or until golden brown all over. Remove the doughnuts from the oil with a slotted spoon, and drain on kitchen paper.

7 While the doughnuts are still warm, poke the handle of a teaspoon into the side of each doughnut, moving the handle around inside the doughnut in a circular motion to make room for the filling.

8 Fill a piping (pastry) bag with the cold custard and squeeze a small amount into each doughnut. Place the sugar for coating on a plate, then toss the doughnuts in the sugar to coat them completely.

Energy 239kcal/1003kJ; Protein 3.8g; Carbohydrate 32.5g, of which sugars 19g; Fat 11.3g, of which saturates 3.4g; Cholesterol 48mg; Calcium 65mg; Fibre 0g; Sodium 106mg.

Baked coffee ring doughnuts

A soft velvety coffee glaze covers these delicious cakey doughnuts. These are lovely served for a mid-morning treat with a cup of coffee, and I like to use any leftovers in home-made tiramisu (broken up instead of the usual sponge fingers) for an unusual variation on the Italian classic dessert.

Makes | 12

non-stick baking oil or melted butter,
  for greasing
100g/3¾oz/scant ½ cup
  butter, softened
150g/5oz/¾ cup caster
  (superfine) sugar
5ml/1 tsp vanilla extract
2 eggs
275g/10oz/2½ cups plain
  (all-purpose) flour
10ml/2 tsp baking powder
15ml/1 tbsp instant coffee
a pinch of salt
150ml/¼ pint/⅔ cup full-fat
  (whole) milk

For the topping
300g/11oz/3¾ cups icing
  (confectioners') sugar
10ml/2 tsp instant coffee
50ml/2fl oz/¼ cup water

1 Preheat the oven to 180°C/350°F/ Gas 4. Spray a 12-cup doughnut baking tin (pan) with non-stick baking oil, or brush with melted butter.

2 Place the softened butter, caster sugar and vanilla extract in a bowl, and whisk together until light and creamy. Add the eggs, one at a time, whisking to make sure the first one is fully incorporated before adding the second.

3 Sift the flour, baking powder, coffee and salt into the mixture and fold in. Add the milk and mix just until it all comes together.

4 Transfer the mixture to a piping (pastry) bag fitted with a round nozzle, then pipe the mixture into the prepared baking tin, dividing it evenly between the cups. Piping the mixture makes it easier to create neat circles, but you can spoon the mixture into the tin, if you prefer.

5 Place the tin in the middle of the oven and bake for 15 minutes, or until golden brown. Remove from the oven and leave to stand for 5 minutes before removing the doughnuts from the tin.

6 For the topping, mix the icing sugar with the coffee and water in a small bowl to make a smooth paste, then spoon over the tops of the doughnuts, while they are still slightly warm.

Energy 311kcal/1314kJ; Protein 3.9g; Carbohydrate 57.7g, of which sugars 40g; Fat 8.8g, of which saturates 5g; Cholesterol 58mg; Calcium 58mg; Fibre 1g; Sodium 74mg.

Chocolate fudge ring doughnuts

These ring doughnuts are especially rich and sweet, with cocoa powder flavouring the dough and a glaze made from sugar and syrup. Fans of chocolate fudge cake will love this indulgent recipe. It uses a choux-style dough rather than a yeast-risen one, and the result is very light and airy.

Makes | 12

75g/3oz/6 tbsp butter
250ml/8fl oz/1 cup water
125g/4¼oz/generous 1 cup plain
  (all-purpose) flour
50g/2oz/½ cup unsweetened
  cocoa powder
a pinch of salt
3 eggs, beaten
about 1 litre/1¾ pints/4 cups
  sunflower oil, for frying

For the glaze
300g/11oz/2¾ cups icing
  (confectioners') sugar
25ml/1½ tbsp water
25ml/1½ tbsp golden
  (light corn) syrup

12 small squares of baking
  parchment

1 Place the butter and water in a pan and bring to the boil. Sift in the flour with the cocoa powder and salt, then mix until it all comes together in a ball. Remove the pan from the heat, then gradually add the eggs, stirring until the mixture forms a thick, smooth paste.

2 Heat the oil for deep-frying in a large, deep pan to 170°C/340°F. Fit a piping (pastry) bag with a star-shaped nozzle, then fill the bag with the doughnut paste. Pipe a ring of paste on to each baking parchment square.

3 Gently lift the doughnuts using the edges of the baking parchment, without disturbing the doughnuts, and slide each one into the hot oil, in batches of 3. (As the paste sticks to the parchment, it is best to place the doughnut and baking parchment into the oil together. The parchment will not burn, and can be removed with tongs or a slotted spoon once it separates from the doughnut.)

4 Cook the doughnuts for 1–2 minutes, turning once, or until lightly browned all over. Remove the doughnuts from the oil with a slotted spoon and drain on kitchen paper.

5 To make the glaze, mix the icing sugar with the water and golden syrup in a bowl until smooth. Dip each doughnut ring into the icing to coat all over, then place on a cooling rack to set.

Energy 283kcal/1192kJ; Protein 3.3g; Carbohydrate 47.7g, of which sugars 33.9g; Fat 10.1g, of which saturates 2.9g; Cholesterol 10mg; Calcium 37mg; Fibre 0.7g; Sodium 143mg.

Chocolate-honey glazed ring doughnuts

Rich chocolatey goodness awaits you in every bite of these honey-sweet doughnuts. The doughnuts are made from a traditional yeast-raised dough, then topped with an indulgent chocolate glaze. For an attractive finishing touch, add chocolate sprinkles or dust with unsweetened cocoa powder.

Makes | 12

225g/8oz/2 cups strong white bread
 flour, plus extra for dusting
7g/¼oz/1½ tsp easy-blend
 (rapid-rise) dried yeast
15ml/1 tbsp caster (superfine) sugar
a pinch of salt
65g/2½oz/5 tbsp butter, cubed
 and chilled
1 egg, beaten
120ml/4fl oz/½ cup full-fat (whole)
 milk, lukewarm
about 1 litre/1¾ pints/4 cups
 sunflower oil, for frying

For the glaze
100g/3¾oz dark (bittersweet)
 chocolate, broken into pieces
100ml/3½fl oz/scant ½ cup
 clear honey
50g/2oz/¼ cup butter

12 small squares of baking
 parchment

1 Sift the flour together with the yeast, sugar and salt into a bowl. Add the butter and rub into the flour mixture using your fingertips. Add the egg and milk, and knead the mixture until it all comes together.

2 Turn out the dough on to a lightly floured work surface and knead for 10 minutes, or until silky smooth. Roll into a ball and place in a clean, lightly greased bowl. Cover with clear film (plastic wrap) and leave to rest in a warm place for about 1 hour, or until doubled in size.

3 Roll out the dough on a lightly floured work surface until it is roughly 1cm/½in thick. Using a doughnut cookie cutter, cut out 12 rings and place each of these on to a baking parchment square. Cover loosely with clear film and leave to stand in a warm place for 30 minutes, until slightly risen.

4 Heat the oil in a large, deep pan to 170ºC/340ºF.

5 Gently lift the doughnuts using the edges of the baking parchment, without disturbing the doughnuts, and slide each one (minus the baking parchment) into the hot oil in batches of 3. Cook them for 30–60 seconds on each side, or until golden brown all over. Remove the doughnuts from the oil with a slotted spoon, and drain on kitchen paper.

6 For the glaze, melt the chocolate, honey and butter together in a non-stick pan over a low heat, stirring until smooth and glossy. Remove from the heat.

7 Spoon the chocolate glaze over the tops of the doughnuts, while they are still slightly warm, allowing it to drizzle down the edges for an attractive finish. Allow to set before serving.

Energy 263kcal/1100kJ; Protein 3g; Carbohydrate 31g, of which sugars 17.9g; Fat 14.9g, of which saturates 6g; Cholesterol 19mg; Calcium 35mg; Fibre 0.3g; Sodium 121mg.

Double chocolate ring doughnuts

These doughnuts are dark and indulgent, and chocolatey through and through. An irresistibly sweet syrupy chocolate glaze smothers the cocoa powder-enriched fried dough, which sets to a lovely shiny finish. Make these before friends arrive and they are sure to be impressed.

Makes | 12

225g/8oz/2 cups plain
  (all-purpose) flour
25g/1oz/¼ cup unsweetened
  cocoa powder
25g/1oz/2 tbsp caster (superfine) sugar
7g/¼oz/1½ tsp easy-blend
  (rapid-rise) dried yeast
a pinch of salt
65g/2½oz/5 tbsp butter, cubed
  and chilled
1 egg
120ml/4fl oz/½ cup full-fat (whole)
  milk, lukewarm
about 1 litre/1¾ pints/4 cups
  sunflower oil, for frying

For the chocolate glaze
100g/3¾oz dark (bittersweet)
  chocolate, broken into pieces
100ml/3½fl oz/scant ½ cup golden
  (light corn) syrup
50g/2oz/¼ cup butter

12 small squares of baking
  parchment

1 Sift the flour together with the cocoa powder, sugar, yeast and salt into a bowl. Add the butter and rub into the flour mixture using your fingertips. Add the egg and milk, and knead the mixture until it all comes together.

2 Turn out the dough on to a lightly floured work surface and knead for 10 minutes, or until silky smooth. Roll into a ball and place in a clean, lightly greased bowl. Cover with clear film (plastic wrap) and leave to rest in a warm place for about 1 hour, or until doubled in size.

3 Cut the dough into 12 even pieces and roll into smooth round balls, placing each one on to a baking parchment square. Cover the dough balls loosely with clear film, then leave to stand in a warm place for 30 minutes.

4 Heat the oil in a large, deep pan to 170°C/340°F.

5 Gently lift the doughnuts using the edges of the baking parchment, without disturbing the doughnuts, and slide each one (minus the baking parchment) into the hot oil in batches of 3. Cook them for 30–60 seconds on each side, or until lightly browned all over. Remove the doughnuts from the oil with a slotted spoon and drain on kitchen paper.

6 To make the chocolate glaze, melt the chocolate, golden syrup and butter together in a non-stick pan over a low heat, stirring until smooth and glossy. Remove from the heat. Pour the glaze into a bowl and dip each doughnut into it, while still slightly warm. Allow to set.

Energy 270kcal/1131kJ; Protein 3.4g; Carbohydrate 31.5g, of which sugars 18.1g; Fat 15.4g, of which saturates 6.2g; Cholesterol 19mg; Calcium 39mg; Fibre 0.6g; Sodium 162mg.

Chocolate de leche ring doughnuts

Chocolate and toffee have always been perfect baking partners and they are no exception in these delicious doughnuts, where a richly textured chocolate dough is topped with sticky toffee. Dulce de leche is usually found with the cans of condensed milk in supermarkets, though any ready-made caramel can be used.

Makes | 12

225g/8oz/2 cups plain
  (all-purpose) flour
25g/1oz/¼ cup unsweetened
  cocoa powder
25g/1oz/2 tbsp caster
  (superfine) sugar
7g/¼oz/1½ tsp easy-blend
  (rapid-rise) dried yeast
a pinch of salt
65g/2½oz/5 tbsp butter, cubed
  and chilled
1 egg
120ml/4fl oz/½ cup full-fat (whole)
  milk, lukewarm
about 1 litre/1¾ pints/4 cups
  sunflower oil, for frying

For the topping
150ml/¼ pint/⅔ cup dulce de leche
  (*see* Cook's Tip)

12 small squares of baking
  parchment

1 Sift the flour together with the cocoa powder, sugar, yeast and salt into a bowl. Add the butter and rub into the flour mixture using your fingertips. Add the egg and milk, and knead the mixture until it all comes together.

2 Turn out the dough on to a lightly floured work surface and knead for 10 minutes, or until silky smooth. Roll into a ball and place in a clean, lightly greased bowl. Cover with clear film (plastic wrap) and leave to rest in a warm place for about 1 hour, or until doubled in size.

COOK'S **TIP**
To make dulce de leche at home, cook a sealed can of condensed milk in a pan of boiling water for 30 minutes. This must be done with care as the can could explode if not continuously immersed in water.

3 Roll out the dough on a lightly floured work surface until it is roughly 1cm/½in thick. Using a doughnut cookie cutter, cut out 12 rings and place each of these on to a baking parchment square. Cover loosely with clear film and leave to stand in a warm place for 30 minutes, until slightly risen.

4 Heat the oil in a large, deep pan to 170°C/340°F. Gently lift the doughnuts using the edges of the baking parchment, without disturbing the doughnuts, and slide each one (minus the baking parchment) into the hot oil in batches of 3. Cook them for 30–60 seconds on each side or until golden brown all over. Remove the doughnuts from the oil with a slotted spoon, and drain on kitchen paper.

5 Spread the dulce de leche over the tops of the doughnuts, while they are still slightly warm.

Energy 249kcal/1044kJ; Protein 4.6g; Carbohydrate 33.2g, of which sugars 20.2g; Fat 11.7g, of which saturates 4g; Cholesterol 19mg; Calcium 104mg; Fibre 0g; Sodium 129mg.

Caramel-filled doughnuts

These doughnuts are filled with thick caramel and can be served with extra caramel on the side for dipping. I have not rolled these in sugar, as I think the caramel filling is sweet enough. Serve with some fruit, such as strawberries, to cut through the caramel and add some freshness to the mix of flavours and textures.

Makes | 12

225g/8oz/2 cups strong white bread
  flour, plus extra for dusting
7g/¼oz/1½ tsp easy-blend
  (rapid-rise) dried yeast
15ml/1 tbsp caster (superfine) sugar
a pinch of salt
65g/2½oz/5 tbsp butter, cubed
  and chilled
1 egg, beaten
120ml/4fl oz/½ cup full-fat (whole)
  milk, lukewarm
about 1 litre/1¾ pints/4 cups
  sunflower oil, for frying

For the filling
150ml/¼ pint/⅔ cup caramel sauce

To serve
a handful of strawberries (optional)

1 Sift the flour together with the yeast, sugar and salt into a bowl. Add the butter and rub into the flour mixture using your fingertips. Add the egg and milk, and knead the mixture until it all comes together.

2 Turn out the dough on to a lightly floured work surface and knead for 10 minutes, or until silky smooth. Roll into a ball and place back into the bowl, cover with clear film (plastic wrap) and leave to rest in a warm place for about 1 hour, or until doubled in size.

3 Cut the dough into 12 even pieces, and roll into smooth round balls. Place each one on to a baking parchment square. Cover loosely with clear film and leave to stand in a warm place for 30 minutes, until slightly risen.

4 Heat the oil in a large, deep pan to 170°C/340°F.

5 Gently lift the doughnuts using the edges of the baking parchment, without disturbing the doughnuts, and slide each one (minus the baking parchment) into the hot oil in batches of 3. Cook them for 30–60 seconds on each side, or until golden brown all over. Remove the doughnuts from the oil with a slotted spoon, and drain on kitchen paper.

6 Poke the handle of a teaspoon into the side of each doughnut, moving the handle around in a circular motion to make room for the filling. Fill a piping (pastry) bag with the caramel, then pipe a small amount into each doughnut, while they are still slightly warm. Serve with strawberries and any leftover caramel.

COOK'S **TIP**
I prefer store-bought caramel sauce to a home-made version here, as it stays soft at room temperature.

Energy 220kcal/923kJ; Protein 2.9g; Carbohydrate 29.4g, of which sugars 16.3g; Fat 10.9g, of which saturates 3.5g; Cholesterol 15mg; Calcium 46mg; Fibre 0g; Sodium 112mg.

Toffee-glazed baked ring doughnuts

Autumnal toffee apples were my inspiration for these toffee-glazed doughnuts. A crunchy toffee coating encases a soft cakey doughnut, giving them a delightful chewiness. Be very careful when handling hot toffee, and keep a bowl of iced water nearby for emergencies.

Makes | 12

non-stick baking oil or melted butter,
  for greasing
100g/3¾oz/scant ½ cup
  butter, softened
150g/5oz/¾ cup caster
  (superfine) sugar
5ml/1 tsp vanilla extract
2 eggs
275g/10oz/2½ cups plain
  (all-purpose) flour
10ml/2 tsp baking powder
a pinch of salt
150ml/¼ pint/⅔ cup full-fat
  (whole) milk

For the toffee glaze
100g/3¾oz/generous ½ cup caster
  (superfine) sugar
50ml/2fl oz/¼ cup water
15ml/1 tbsp golden (light corn) syrup

1 Preheat the oven to 180°C/350°F/ Gas 4. Spray a 12-cup doughnut baking tin (pan) with non-stick baking oil, or brush with melted butter.

2 Place the softened butter, sugar and vanilla extract in a bowl and whisk together until light and creamy. Add the eggs, one at a time, whisking to make sure the first one is fully incorporated before adding the second.

3 Sift the flour, baking powder and salt into the mixture, and fold in. Add the milk, and mix with a spatula just until it all comes together.

4 Transfer the mixture to a piping bag fitted with a round nozzle, then pipe the mixture into the prepared baking tin, dividing it evenly between the cups. Piping the mixture makes it easier to create neat circles, but you can spoon the mixture into the tin, if you prefer.

5 Place the tin in the middle of the oven and bake for 15 minutes, or until golden brown. Remove from the oven and leave to stand for 5 minutes before removing the doughnuts from the tin.

6 Meanwhile, make the toffee glaze. Heat the sugar and water in a heavy pan until the sugar dissolves, then add the syrup and bring to a rolling boil. Cook, stirring, for 5 minutes over a medium-high heat, or until a small spoonful of toffee hardens when dunked into cold water. Remove the pan from the heat.

7 Drizzle the toffee over the tops of the doughnuts, while they are still slightly warm, then leave to set.

Energy 171kcal/718kJ; Protein 1.8g; Carbohydrate 23.4g, of which sugars 23.4g; Fat 8.5g, of which saturates 5g; Cholesterol 58mg; Calcium 28mg; Fibre 0g; Sodium 74mg.

Salted caramel doughnuts

The classic sweet and salty flavour combination works perfectly in these salted caramel doughnuts, with the sea salt crystals giving a little crunch and cutting the sweetness of the caramel. I recommend using reduced (low) sodium salt flakes for this recipe, which are available in most supermarkets.

Makes | 12

225g/8oz/2 cups strong white bread flour, plus extra for dusting
7g/¼oz/1½ tsp easy-blend (rapid-rise) dried yeast
15ml/1 tbsp caster (superfine) sugar
a pinch of salt
65g/2½oz/5 tbsp butter, cubed and chilled
1 egg, beaten
120ml/4fl oz/½ cup full-fat (whole) milk, lukewarm
about 1 litre/1¾ pints/4 cups sunflower oil, for frying

For the filling
60–75ml/4–5 tbsp dulce de leche

For the topping
100ml/3½fl oz/scant ½ cup dulce de leche
15g/½oz sea salt flakes

12 small squares of baking parchment

1 Sift the flour together with the yeast, sugar and pinch of salt into a bowl. Add the butter and rub into the flour mixture using your fingertips. Add the egg and milk, and knead the mixture until it all comes together.

2 Turn out the dough on to a lightly floured work surface and knead for 10 minutes, or until silky smooth. Roll into a ball and place back into the bowl, cover with clear film (plastic wrap) and leave to rest in a warm place for about 1 hour, or until doubled in size.

3 Cut the dough into 12 even pieces and roll into smooth round balls, placing each one on to a baking parchment square. Cover loosely with clear film, and leave to stand in a warm place for 30 minutes, until slightly risen.

4 Heat the oil in a large, deep pan to 170°C/340°F.

5 Gently lift the doughnuts using the edges of the baking parchment, without disturbing the doughnuts, and slide each one (minus the baking parchment) into the hot oil in batches of 3, cooking them for 30–60 seconds on each side or until golden brown all over. Remove the doughnuts from the oil with a slotted spoon and drain on kitchen paper.

6 While the doughnuts are still warm, poke the handle of a teaspoon into the side of each doughnut, moving the handle around inside the doughnut in a circular motion to make room for the filling.

7 Fill a piping (pastry) bag with the dulce de leche for the filling, and squeeze a small amount into each doughnut, while the doughnuts are still slightly warm. For the topping, spread a little dulce de leche over the top of each doughnut using a palette knife or metal spatula, then sprinkle with some sea salt flakes.

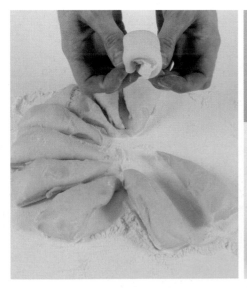

Energy 262kcal/1102kJ; Protein 5g; Carbohydrate 35.5g, of which sugars 22.5g; Fat 12.1g, of which saturates 4.2g; Cholesterol 20mg; Calcium 116mg; Fibre 0g; Sodium 463mg.

Iced eggless ring doughnuts

For those who can't eat eggs, this is the ideal treat – a tasty doughnut, without eggs, fried to perfection and topped with a buttery icing and colourful sprinkles for a fun finish. You can take the eggless dough and pair it with any other topping or filling in this book, of course.

Makes | 12

225g/8oz/2 cups strong white bread flour, plus extra for dusting
7g/¼oz/1½ tsp easy-blend (rapid-rise) dried yeast
15ml/1 tbsp caster (superfine) sugar
a pinch of salt
65g/2½oz/5 tbsp butter, cubed and chilled
120ml/4fl oz/½ cup full-fat (whole) milk, lukewarm
about 1 litre/1¾ pints/4 cups sunflower oil, for frying

For the glaze and decoration
300g/11oz/2¾ cups icing (confectioners') sugar
25ml/1½ tbsp water
25g/1oz/2 tbsp butter, melted
60ml/4 tbsp sprinkles

12 small squares of baking parchment

1 Sift the flour together with the yeast, sugar and salt into a bowl. Add the butter and rub into the flour mixture using your fingertips. Add the milk, and knead the mixture until it all comes together.

2 Turn out the dough on to a lightly floured work surface, and knead for 10 minutes, or until silky smooth. Roll into a ball and place back into the bowl, cover with clear film (plastic wrap) and leave to rest in a warm place for about 1 hour, or until doubled in size.

3 Roll out the dough on a lightly floured work surface until it is roughly 1cm/½in thick. Using a doughnut cookie cutter, cut out 12 rings and place each of these on to a baking parchment square. Cover loosely with clear film and leave to stand in a warm place for 30 minutes, until slightly risen.

4 Heat the oil in a large, deep pan to 170°C/340°F.

5 Gently lift the doughnuts using the edges of the baking parchment, without disturbing the doughnuts, and slide each one (minus the baking parchment) into the hot oil in batches of 3. Cook them for 30–60 seconds on each side or until golden brown all over. Remove the doughnuts from the oil with a slotted spoon, and drain on kitchen paper.

6 For the glaze, mix the icing sugar with the water and butter, then spoon over the doughnuts, while they are still slightly warm. Cover with sprinkles, then allow to set before serving.

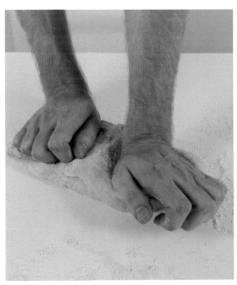

Energy 301kcal/1267kJ; Protein 0.6g; Carbohydrate 50.3g, of which sugars 35.1g; Fat 11.3g, of which saturates 3.7g; Cholesterol 14mg; Calcium 33mg; Fibre 0.1g; Sodium 114mg.

Gluten-free baked ring doughnuts

For those intolerant to gluten, this recipe never fails to please. I'm not gluten intolerant myself, but I do love these doughnuts. I have given these a chocolate topping, but you can use any of the toppings or glazes from this book instead. Alternatively, just toss them in sugar.

Makes | 12

non-stick baking oil (*see* Cook's Tip)
  or melted butter, for greasing
100g/3¾oz/scant ½ cup
  butter, softened
150g/5oz/¾ cup caster
  (superfine) sugar
5ml/1 tsp vanilla extract
2 eggs
300g/11oz/2¾ cups gluten-free
  plain (all-purpose) flour
5ml/1 tsp xanthan gum powder
10ml/2 tsp gluten-free baking powder
a pinch of salt
150ml/¼ pint/⅔ cup full-fat
  (whole) milk

For the topping
100g/3¾oz dark (bittersweet)
  chocolate, broken into pieces
100ml/3½fl oz/scant ½ cup golden
  (light corn) syrup
50g/2oz/¼ cup butter

1 Preheat the oven to 180°C/350°F/ Gas 4. Spray a 12-cup doughnut baking tin (pan) with non-stick baking oil, or brush with melted butter.

2 Place the softened butter, sugar and vanilla extract in a bowl and whisk together until light and creamy. Add the eggs, one at a time, whisking to make sure the first one is fully incorporated before adding the second.

3 Sift the flour, xanthan gum powder, baking powder and salt into the mixture, and fold in. Add the milk and mix just until it all comes together.

4 Transfer the mixture to a piping bag fitted with a round nozzle, then pipe the mixture into the prepared baking tin, dividing it evenly between the cups. Piping the mixture makes it easier to create neat circles, but you can spoon the mixture into the tin, if you prefer.

COOK'S **TIP**
Some baking oil sprays contain flour, so check that you have a gluten-free brand before using.

5 Place the baking tin in the middle of the oven and bake for 15 minutes, or until golden brown. Remove from the oven and leave to stand for 5 minutes before removing the doughnuts from the tin.

6 Meanwhile, for the chocolate icing, place the chocolate, syrup and butter in a non-stick pan, and melt over a low heat, stirring until smooth and glossy.

7 Spoon the glaze over the doughnuts, while they are still slightly warm, allowing the glaze to drizzle down the sides. Place on a cooling rack and allow to set.

Energy 346kcal/1456kJ; Protein 5.4g; Carbohydrate 51.4g, of which sugars 26g; Fat 14.6g, of which saturates 8.6g; Cholesterol 67mg; Calcium 90mg; Fibre 1.6g; Sodium 267mg.

Wholemeal ring doughnuts

These doughnuts offer a more substantial and wholesome alternative to plain doughnuts. I like the texture of wholemeal flour, and it is a little healthier too. For a different dusting, I've covered these in crunchy brown sugar, but feel free to use white sugar instead, if you prefer.

Makes | 12

225g/8oz/2 cups strong wholemeal (whole-wheat) bread flour, plus extra for dusting
7g/¼oz/1½ tsp easy-blend (rapid-rise) dried yeast
15ml/1 tbsp caster (superfine) sugar
a pinch of salt
65g/2½oz/5 tbsp butter, cubed and chilled
1 egg, beaten
120ml/4fl oz/½ cup full-fat (whole) milk, lukewarm
about 1 litre/1¾ pints/4 cups sunflower oil, for frying

For coating
115g/4oz/generous ½ cup demerara (raw) sugar

VARIATION
Try these without the sugar coating. Slice them in half and spread with low-fat cream cheese instead, rather like a bagel.

---

1 Sift the flour together with the yeast, sugar and salt into a bowl. Add the butter and rub into the flour mixture using your fingertips. Add the egg and milk, and knead the mixture until it all comes together.

2 Turn out the dough on to a lightly floured work surface and knead for 10 minutes, or until silky smooth. Roll into a ball and place in a clean, lightly greased bowl. Cover with clear film (plastic wrap) and leave to rest in a warm place for about 1 hour, or until doubled in size.

3 Roll out the dough on a lightly floured work surface until it is roughly 1cm/½in thick. Using a doughnut cookie cutter, cut out 12 rings and place each of these on to a baking parchment square. Cover loosely with clear film and leave to stand in a warm place for 30 minutes, until slightly risen.

4 Heat the oil in a large, deep pan to 170°C/340°F.

5 Gently lift the doughnuts using the edges of the baking parchment, without disturbing the doughnuts, and slide each one (minus the baking parchment) into the hot oil in batches of 3. Cook them for 30–60 seconds on each side or until golden brown all over. Remove the doughnuts from the oil with a slotted spoon, and drain on kitchen paper.

6 Place the demerara sugar on a plate, and toss the doughnuts in the sugar, while they are still slightly warm, to coat them completely.

Energy 203kcal/853kJ; Protein 2.6g; Carbohydrate 29.4g, of which sugars 16.3g; Fat 9.2g, of which saturates 2.4g; Cholesterol 10mg; Calcium 34mg; Fibre 3.5g; Sodium 95mg.

Doughnut-hole pops

These doughnut holes were originally made from the bits of dough that remained after the ring shapes had been cut out. These can be served in a bowl, but I like to place them on sticks and serve them as doughnut hole pops! I find that three holes on each stick is a good serving size.

Makes | 12

225g/8oz/2 cups strong white bread
  flour, plus extra for dusting
7g/¼oz/1½ tsp easy-blend
  (rapid-rise) dried yeast
15ml/1 tbsp caster (superfine) sugar
a pinch of salt
65g/2½oz/5 tbsp butter, cubed
  and chilled
1 egg, beaten
120ml/4fl oz/½ cup full-fat (whole)
  milk, lukewarm
about 1 litre/1¾ pints/4 cups
  sunflower oil, for frying

For sprinkling
115g/4oz/generous ½ cup caster
  (superfine) sugar

1 large sheet of baking parchment
12 wooden skewers

1 Sift the flour together with the yeast, sugar and salt into a bowl. Add the butter and rub into the flour mixture using your fingertips. Add the egg and milk, and knead the mixture until it all comes together.

2 Turn out the dough on to a lightly floured work surface and knead for 10 minutes, or until silky smooth. Roll into a ball and place in a clean, lightly greased bowl. Cover with clear film (plastic wrap) and leave to rest in a warm place for about 1 hour, or until doubled in size.

3 Cut the dough into 36 even pieces, and roll each piece into a smooth round ball. Place all the balls on to a large sheet of baking parchment. Cover loosely with clear film and leave to stand in a warm place for 30 minutes, until slightly risen.

4 Heat the oil in a large, deep pan to 170°C/340°F.

5 Gently lift the doughnuts using the edges of the baking parchment, without disturbing the doughnuts, and slide each one (minus the baking parchment) into the hot oil in batches of 6–8. Cook them for 30–60 seconds on each side or until golden brown all over. Remove the doughnuts from the oil with a slotted spoon, and drain on kitchen paper.

6 Take a wooden skewer and push 3 doughnut holes on to it, then repeat with the remaining skewers and doughnut holes. Sprinkle the pops with sugar to coat all over, while still slightly warm. (Alternatively, just sprinkle the doughnut holes with sugar and serve.)

Energy 203kcal/853kJ; Protein 2.6g; Carbohydrate 29.4g, of which sugars 16.3g; Fat 9.2g, of which saturates 2.4g; Cholesterol 10mg; Calcium 34mg; Fibre 0g; Sodium 95mg.

Doughnut-hole croquembouche

For a true showstopper, try making this doughnut hole croquembouche for your next party. It will certainly impress your guests. Be very careful with hot caramel, as it can cause serious burns.

Serves | 24

450g/1lb/4 cups strong white bread flour, plus extra for dusting
14g/½oz/1 tbsp easy-blend (rapid-rise) dried yeast
60ml/4 tbsp caster (superfine) sugar
2.5ml/½ tsp salt
125g/4¼oz/8½ tbsp butter, cubed and chilled
2 eggs, beaten
225ml/7½fl oz/scant 1 cup full-fat (whole) milk, lukewarm
about 1 litre/1¾ pints/4 cups sunflower oil, for frying

For the caramel
300g/11oz/1½ cups caster (superfine) sugar
200ml/7fl oz/scant 1 cup water
50ml/2fl oz/¼ cup glucose syrup

For decorating
white and pink sugar flowers

2 large sheets of baking parchment

1 Sift the flour together with the yeast, caster sugar and salt into a bowl. Add the butter and rub into the flour mixture using your fingertips. Add the eggs and milk, and knead the mixture until it all comes together.

2 Turn out the dough on to a lightly floured work surface, and knead for 10 minutes, or until silky smooth. Roll into a ball and place back into the bowl, cover with clear film (plastic wrap) and leave to rest in a warm place for about 1 hour, or until doubled in size.

3 Cut the dough into 72 even pieces, and roll into smooth round balls. Place all the balls on to the baking parchment sheets. Cover loosely with clear film and leave to stand in a warm place for 30 minutes, or until slightly risen.

4 Heat the oil in a large, deep pan to 170°C/340°F. Gently lift the doughnuts using the edges of the baking parchment, without disturbing the doughnuts, and slide each one (minus the baking parchment) into the hot oil in batches of 6–9, cooking them for 30–60 seconds on each side, or until golden brown all over. Remove the doughnuts from the oil with a slotted spoon and drain on kitchen paper.

5 Prepare an ice-water bath. For the caramel, place the sugar, water and glucose syrup in a pan and bring to a rolling boil over medium heat, without stirring. Continue to boil the mixture until it reaches 135°C/275°F on a sugar thermometer, then remove from the heat and plunge the base of the pan into the ice-water bath to arrest the cooking.

6 Dip one side of a doughnut hole into the caramel, and then place it, caramel side down, on to a serving plate. Repeat with more doughnut holes to create a filled circle. Continue in the same way, building up another layer, slightly smaller than the first. Keep adding layers in the same way until you have formed a pyramid. If the caramel starts to solidify, briefly place the pan back over a low heat to melt it.

7 Use the remaining caramel to make the spun sugar. Position a wooden rolling pin at the edge of a table or work surface so that it partly sticks out over the floor. Cover the floor beneath with baking parchment. Dip a spoon into the hot caramel and flick this over the rolling pin. The caramel will form long strands in the air between the rolling pin and the floor. Gently lift the strands off the rolling pin and wrap them around the pyramid, then decorate with sugar flowers.

Energy 207kcal/871kJ; Protein 2.4g; Carbohydrate 32.5g, of which sugars 19.6g; Fat 8.4g, of which saturates 2.2g; Cholesterol 9mg; Calcium 32mg; Fibre 0g; Sodium 90mg.

Doughnuts around the World

There are almost as many varieties of doughnut as there are countries, and some are age old recipes that have been passed from generation to generation. Doughnuts tend to be served at festivals and celebrations around the world, symbolizing how culinary and cultural traditions bring families and communities together.

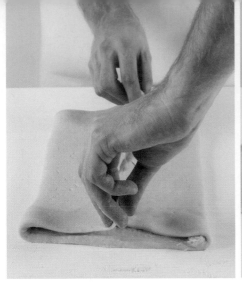  

Yum Yums

These classic American twists are made from dough that is brushed with melted butter before shaping and frying, making them extra crisp and tasty – naughty but nice at its best. To ring the changes, add finely grated citrus rind to the glaze or perhaps a dash of rose water to elevate the glaze slightly.

Makes | 12

300g/11oz/2¾ cups plain
  (all-purpose) flour, plus extra
  for dusting
7g/¼oz/1½ tsp easy-blend
  (rapid-rise) dried yeast
a pinch of salt
30ml/2 tbsp caster (superfine) sugar
65g/2½oz/5 tbsp butter, cubed
  and chilled
1 egg, beaten
150ml/¼ pint/⅔ cup full-fat
  (whole) milk
65g/2½oz/5 tbsp butter, very soft,
  for brushing
about 1 litre/1¾ pints/4 cups
  sunflower oil, for frying

For the glaze
300g/11oz/2¾ cups icing
  (confectioners') sugar
50ml/2fl oz/¼ cup water

12 small rectangles of baking
  parchment

1 Sift the flour together with the yeast, salt and sugar into a bowl. Add the chilled butter, and rub in until slightly crumbly.

2 Add the egg and milk, and knead the mixture for 10 minutes, then shape into a ball. Place in a lightly oiled bowl, cover with clear film (plastic wrap) and leave to stand at room temperature for 1 hour, or until doubled in size.

3 Roll out the dough on a lightly floured work surface to a 20cm x 40cm/8in x 16in rectangle that is roughly 1cm/½in thick. Brush all over with a little of the very soft butter.

4 Take one of the short ends of the dough, and fold it to the centre, then repeat with the other side of the dough. Now fold the dough in half, as if closing a book. Allow the dough to rest for 15 minutes, covered in clear film, at room temperature.

5 Roll out the dough again to a 20cm x 40cm/8in x 16in rectangle, then brush with more softened butter and repeat the folding process. Roll out again to a 20cm x 40cm/8in x 16in rectangle.

6 Using a sharp knife, cut the dough crossways into 12 even strips. Use a knife to cut lengthways through the centre of each strip, leaving the ends intact. Twist the strip, pressing the ends together to seal. Place each yum yum twist on to a baking parchment rectangle.

7 Heat the oil in a large, deep pan to 170°C/340°F.

8 Gently lift the doughnut twists using the edges of the baking parchment, without disturbing the twists, and slide each one (minus the baking parchment) into the hot oil in batches of 3, cooking them for 30–60 seconds on each side, or until golden brown all over. Remove the doughnut twists from the oil with a slotted spoon and drain on kitchen paper.

9 Make the glaze by mixing the icing sugar and water together in a small bowl until smooth and combined. Brush the glaze over the tops of the yum yums, while they are still slightly warm, then leave to set on a wire rack before serving.

Energy 326kcal/1372kJ; Protein 3.4g; Carbohydrate 52.9g, of which sugars 34.6g; Fat 12.6g, of which saturates 3.3g; Cholesterol 14mg; Calcium 43mg; Fibre 0g; Sodium 133mg.

Apple fritters

These are my version of apple fritters using freshly grated apple mixed into a batter and lightly fried. This is the way I grew up eating them, and they bring back happy memories of childhood comfort food. Try these fritters drizzled with vanilla custard, for a scrumptious dessert.

Makes | 12

2 eating apples, peeled and cored
140g/4¾oz/scant 1¼ cups strong
   white bread flour, plus extra
   for dusting
140g/4¾oz/scant 1¼ cups strong
   wholemeal (whole-wheat)
   bread flour
5ml/1 tsp baking powder
a pinch of salt
275ml/9fl oz/generous 1 cup
   water, lukewarm
15ml/1 tbsp clear honey
1 egg
2.5ml/½ tsp ground nutmeg
about 30ml/2 tbsp sunflower oil,
   for frying
golden (light corn) syrup, to serve

1 Grate the apples coarsely, then squeeze out any excess moisture using some kitchen paper. Set aside on more kitchen paper while you quickly make the batter. Do not grate them in advance, as they will turn brown.

2 Sift the strong white bread flour and wholemeal flour together with the baking powder and salt into a large mixing bowl.

3 Add the water, honey and egg, and stir until combined.

4 Add the grated apples to the batter, along with the nutmeg, and stir to mix until well combined.

5 Heat the oil in a large frying pan. Working in batches of 3, drop about 30ml/2 tbsp of batter for each fritter into the hot oil, and cook for 30–60 seconds on each side, or until golden brown all over.

6 Remove the cooked fritters from the oil using a slotted spoon or fish slice, and drain on kitchen paper. Keep warm while you cook the remaining batches.

7 Serve the fritters warm, drizzled with golden syrup.

Energy 113kcal/478kJ; Protein 3.3g; Carbohydrate 20g, of which sugars 3.3g; Fat 2.8g, of which saturates 0.4g; Cholesterol 19mg; Calcium 35mg; Fibre 1.9g; Sodium 8mg.

Churros with chocolate dip

These Spanish fried treats are popular the world over, and are fun for kids and adults alike. Served with a hot chocolate dip for dunking, they can be coated with a variety of flavoured sugars. Here I have gone for the traditional addition of cinnamon, but you can use other spices, if you like.

Makes |24

75g/3oz/6 tbsp butter
250ml/8fl oz/1 cup water
140g/4¾oz/scant 1¼ cups plain
 (all-purpose) flour
a pinch of salt
3 eggs, beaten
about 1 litre/1¾ pints/4 cups
 sunflower oil, for frying

For coating
90ml/6 tbsp caster (superfine) sugar
5ml/1 tsp ground cinnamon

For the chocolate dip
100g/3¾oz dark (bittersweet)
 chocolate, broken into pieces
100ml/3½fl oz/scant ½ cup golden
 (light corn) syrup
50g/2oz/¼ cup butter

1 First, make the chocolate dip. Melt the chocolate, syrup and butter together in a non-stick pan over a medium heat, stirring until smooth and glossy. Remove from the heat and set aside while you make the churros, stirring occasionally.

2 Place the butter and water in a pan and bring to the boil. Sift in the flour and salt, then mix until it all comes together in a ball. Remove from the heat, then gradually add the eggs, stirring until the mixture forms a thick, smooth paste.

3 Heat the oil in a large, deep pan to 170°C/340°F. Fit a piping (pastry) bag with a star-shaped nozzle, then fill the bag with the paste. Pipe 10–15cm/ 4–6in lengths of paste into the hot oil and cook them, in batches of 3, for 1–2 minutes, turning once, until golden brown all over. Remove the churros from the oil with a slotted spoon and drain on kitchen paper.

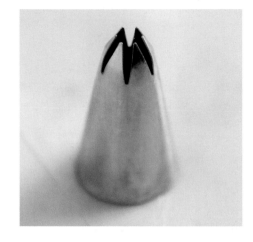

4 For coating, mix the sugar with the cinnamon and sprinkle over the churros, while they are still slightly warm, to coat them completely. Serve with the chocolate dip.

VARIATION
For a chocolate-orange dipping sauce, just add the finely grated rind of an orange.

Energy 130kcal/547kJ; Protein 1.3g; Carbohydrate 17.6g, of which sugars 12.4g; Fat 6.6g, of which saturates 2.7g; Cholesterol 9mg; Calcium 16mg; Fibre 0.1g; Sodium 62mg.

Crullers

A French favourite, these crullers are very similar to churros but are piped as rings and covered in a lovely honey glaze. Using a star-shaped nozzle makes the ridged edges of the crullers very crisp, and I love how the crunchy exterior gives way to a sumptuously soft middle.

Makes | 12

75g/3oz/6 tbsp butter
250ml/8fl oz/1 cup water
175g/6oz/1½ cups plain
  (all-purpose) flour
a pinch of salt
3 eggs, beaten
1 egg white, beaten
about 1 litre/1¾ pints/4 cups
  sunflower oil, for frying

For the glaze
300g/11oz/2¾ cups icing
  (confectioners') sugar
50ml/2fl oz/¼ cup water
25ml/1½ tbsp clear honey

12 small squares of baking
  parchment

1 Place the butter and water in a pan and bring to the boil. Sift in the flour with the salt, then mix until it all comes together in a ball. Take the pan off the heat, then gradually add the eggs and egg white, stirring until the mixture forms a thick, smooth paste.

2 Heat the oil in a large, deep pan to 170ºC/340ºF. Fit a piping (pastry) bag with a star-shaped nozzle, then fill the bag with the paste. Pipe a ring of paste on to each baking parchment square.

3 Gently lift the crullers using the edges of the baking parchment, without disturbing the doughnuts, and slide each one into the hot oil, in batches of 3. As the paste sticks to the parchment, it is best to place the crullers and parchment into the oil together. The parchment will not burn, and can be removed with tongs or a slotted spoon once it separates from the cruller.

4 Cook the crullers for 1–2 minutes, turning once, or until lightly browned all over. Remove the crullers from the oil with a slotted spoon, and drain on kitchen paper.

5 For the glaze, mix the icing sugar, water and honey together in a bowl until smooth and combined. Dip the crullers in the glaze to coat completely, while still slightly warm, then leave to set before serving.

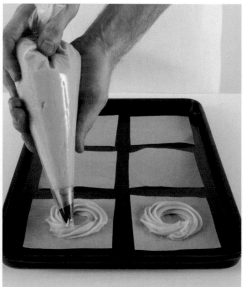

Energy 346kcal/1458kJ; Protein 3.8g; Carbohydrate 56.2g, of which sugars 37.2g; Fat 13.4g, of which saturates 3.5g; Cholesterol 14mg; Calcium 53mg; Fibre 0g; Sodium 139mg.

Bombolini

These Italian beauties are much-loved snacks for children in Italy. They can be filled with custard, chocolate or jam, but here I have chosen chocolate hazelnut spread. You only need to pipe a small amount of spread into the middle of the doughnuts, as there is also a layer on top! Top with chopped peanuts for textural variation.

Makes | 12

225g/8oz/2 cups strong white bread
   flour, plus extra for dusting
7g/¼oz/1½ tsp easy-blend
   (rapid-rise) dried yeast
15ml/1 tbsp caster (superfine) sugar
a pinch of salt
65g/2½oz/5 tbsp butter, cubed
   and chilled
1 egg, beaten
120ml/4fl oz/½ cup full-fat (whole)
   milk, lukewarm
about 1 litre/1¾ pints/4 cups
   sunflower oil, for frying

For the filling and topping
225g/8oz/1 cup chocolate
   hazelnut spread
50g/2oz/½ cup peanuts,
   roughly chopped

12 small squares of baking
   parchment

1 Sift the flour together with the yeast, sugar and salt into a bowl. Add the butter and rub into the flour mixture using your fingertips. Add the egg and milk, and knead the mixture until it all comes together.

2 Turn out the dough on to a lightly floured work surface and knead for 10 minutes, or until silky smooth. Roll into a ball and place back into the bowl, cover with clear film (plastic wrap) and leave to rest in a warm place for about 1 hour, or until doubled in size.

3 Cut the dough into 12 even pieces and roll into smooth round balls, placing each one on to a baking parchment square. Cover loosely with clear film and leave to stand in a warm place for 30 minutes, or until slightly risen.

4 Heat the oil in a large, deep pan to 170°C/340°F.

5 Gently lift the doughnuts using the edges of the baking parchment, without disturbing the doughnuts, and slide each one (minus the baking parchment) into the hot oil in batches of 3, cooking them for 30–60 seconds on each side or until golden brown all over. Remove the doughnuts from the oil with a slotted spoon and drain on kitchen paper.

6 While the doughnuts are still warm, poke the handle of a teaspoon into the side of each doughnut, moving the handle around inside the doughnut in a circular motion to make room for the filling.

7 Fill a piping (pastry) bag with half of the chocolate and hazelnut spread, and squeeze a small amount into each doughnut. Spread the remaining chocolate and hazelnut spread on to the tops of the doughnuts, then decorate with chopped peanuts.

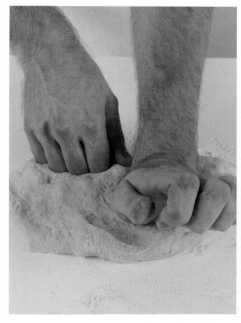  

Energy 292kcal/1220kJ; Protein 4.7g; Carbohydrate 31.2g, of which sugars 17.7g; Fat 17.3g, of which saturates 4.5g; Cholesterol 10mg; Calcium 58mg; Fibre 0.2g; Sodium 104mg.

Malasadas

These are classic Portuguese doughnuts, similar to a plain doughnut, but slightly richer thanks to the addition of sweetened condensed milk. They are dropped free-form into the oil, and they have a crunchy outside and a super fluffy inside. This is my version, and I've used nutmeg in the sugar, to add a special touch.

Makes 12

300g/11oz/2¾ cups strong white
  bread flour, plus extra for dusting
7g/¼oz/1½ tsp easy-blend
  (rapid-rise) dried yeast
30ml/2 tbsp caster (superfine) sugar
a pinch of salt
80g/3¾oz/6½ tbsp butter, cubed
  and chilled
3 eggs, beaten
300ml/½ pint/1¼ cups sweetened
  condensed milk, at room temperature
about 1 litre/1¾ pints/4 cups
  sunflower oil, for frying

For coating
60ml/4 tbsp icing
  (confectioners') sugar
1.5ml/¼ tsp ground nutmeg

12 small squares of baking
  parchment

1 Sift the flour together with the yeast, caster sugar and salt into a bowl. Add the butter and rub into the flour mixture using your fingertips. Add the eggs and condensed milk, and mix until combined.

2 Heat the oil for deep-frying in a large, deep pan to 170°C/340°F. Using an ice cream scoop or two tablespoons, form a ball of batter and drop it gently into the hot oil. Repeat with the remaining batter, frying the malasadas in batches of 3, for 30–60 seconds on each side, or until golden brown all over. Remove the doughnuts from the oil with a slotted spoon and drain on kitchen paper.

3 While the malasadas are still warm, mix the icing sugar with the nutmeg on a plate, then toss the malasadas in the mixture.

COOK'S **TIP**
These are traditionally eaten the day before Lent starts, as a way of using all the sugar and flour from the storecupboard, similar to the tradition of making pancakes on Shrove Tuesday.

Energy 321kcal/1346kJ; Protein 4.6g; Carbohydrate 40.5g, of which sugars 16.7g; Fat 16.7g, of which saturates 4.3g; Cholesterol 18mg; Calcium 58mg; Fibre 0g; Sodium 172mg.

Berliner

These German favourites are traditional jam doughnuts, with lovely flavour additions to the dough. These can be had at any time of year in Germany, but mainly during the Carnival celebrations. My secret ingredients here are vanilla extract and almond extract, and this is the way my grandmother made them.

Makes | 12

225g/8oz/2 cups strong white bread flour, plus extra for dusting
7g/¼oz/1½ tsp easy-blend (rapid-rise) dried yeast
15ml/1 tbsp caster (superfine) sugar
a pinch of salt
65g/2½oz/5 tbsp butter, cubed and chilled
1 egg, beaten
120ml/4fl oz/½ cup full-fat (whole) milk, lukewarm
5ml/1 tsp vanilla extract
1.5ml/¼ tsp almond extract
about 1 litre/1¾ pints/4 cups sunflower oil, for frying

For the filling and coating
150g/5oz/½ cup raspberry jam
115g/4oz/generous ½ cup granulated (white) sugar

12 small squares of baking parchment

1 Sift the flour together with the yeast, sugar and salt into a bowl. Add the butter and rub into the flour mixture using your fingertips. Add the egg, milk, vanilla extract and almond extract, and knead the mixture until it all comes together.

2 Turn out the dough on to a lightly floured work surface and knead for 10 minutes, or until silky smooth. Roll into a ball and place back into the bowl, cover with clear film (plastic wrap) and leave to rest in a warm place for about 1 hour, or until doubled in size.

3 Cut the dough into 12 even pieces and roll into smooth round balls, placing each one on to a baking parchment square. Cover loosely with clear film and leave to stand in a warm place for 30 minutes, or until slightly risen.

4 Heat the oil in a large, deep pan to 170°C/340°F.

5 Gently lift the doughnuts using the edges of the baking parchment, without disturbing the doughnuts, and slide each one (minus the baking parchment) into the hot oil in batches of 3, cooking them for 30–60 seconds on each side or until golden brown all over. Remove the doughnuts from the oil with a slotted spoon and drain on kitchen paper.

6 While the doughnuts are still warm, poke the handle of a teaspoon into the side of each doughnut, moving the handle around inside the doughnut in a circular motion to make room for the filling.

7 Fill a piping (pastry) bag with the jam, and squeeze a small amount into each doughnut.

8 To coat the doughnuts, place the sugar on a plate, and toss the doughnuts in it, to coat them completely.

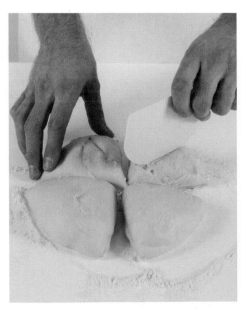

Energy 236kcal/992kJ; Protein 2.6g; Carbohydrate 38g, of which sugars 24.9g; Fat 9.2g, of which saturates 2.4g; Cholesterol 10mg; Calcium 35mg; Fibre 0g; Sodium 98mg.

Krapfen

Krapfen are similar to Berliner, but are usually filled with delicious apricot jam and sprinkled with powdery icing sugar instead of caster sugar. It is difficult not to get icing sugar all over your face when eating these – making them a firm favourite among German children.

Makes | 12

225g/8oz/2 cups strong white bread
   flour, plus extra for dusting
7g/¼oz/1½ tsp easy-blend
   (rapid-rise) dried yeast
15ml/1 tbsp caster (superfine) sugar
a pinch of salt
65g/2½oz/5 tbsp butter, cubed
   and chilled
1 egg, beaten
120ml/4fl oz/½ cup full-fat (whole)
   milk, lukewarm
5ml/1 tsp vanilla extract
about 1 litre/1¾pints/4 cups
   sunflower oil, for frying

For the filling and sprinkling
150g/5oz/½ cup apricot jam
icing (confectioners') sugar,
   for sprinkling

12 small squares of baking
   parchment

1 Sift the flour together with the yeast, caster sugar and salt into a bowl. Add the butter and rub into the flour mixture using your fingertips. Add the egg, milk and vanilla extract, and knead the mixture until it all comes together.

2 Turn out the dough on to a lightly floured work surface and knead for 10 minutes, or until silky smooth. Roll into a ball and place back into the bowl, cover with clear film (plastic wrap) and leave to rest in a warm place for about 1 hour, or until doubled in size.

3 Cut the dough into 12 even pieces and roll into smooth round balls, placing each one on to a baking parchment square. Cover loosely with clear film and leave to stand in a warm place for 30 minutes, or until slightly risen.

4 Heat the oil in a large, deep pan to 170°C/340°F.

5 Gently lift the doughnuts using the edges of the baking parchment, without disturbing the doughnuts, and slide each one (minus the baking parchment) into the hot oil in batches of 3. Cook them for 30–60 seconds on each side, or until golden brown all over. Remove the doughnuts from the oil with a slotted spoon and drain on kitchen paper.

6 While the doughnuts are still warm, poke the handle of a teaspoon into the side of each doughnut, moving the handle around inside the doughnut in a circular motion to make room for the filling.

7 Fill a piping (pastry) bag with the apricot jam and squeeze a small amount into each doughnut.

8 Sprinkle the krapfen with icing sugar on both sides, to coat them completely.

Energy 198kcal/832kJ; Protein 2.6g; Carbohydrate 28g, of which sugars 14.9g; Fat 9.2g, of which saturates 2.4g; Cholesterol 10mg; Calcium 32mg; Fibre 0g; Sodium 100mg.

Oliebollen

Oliebollen are commonly considered to be the 'original' doughnut. Literally 'oil balls', they are small puffs of fried dough, a little smaller than the usual doughnut. They are known as Dutch doughnuts or Dutchies in other countries. They can be eaten filled or unfilled, but always covered in either caster sugar or icing sugar.

Makes | 12

300g/11oz/2¾ cups strong white
  bread flour, plus extra for dusting
7g/¼oz/1½ tsp easy-blend
  (rapid-rise) dried yeast
15ml/1 tbsp caster (superfine) sugar
a pinch of salt
450ml/¾pint/scant 2 cups full-fat
  (whole) milk, lukewarm
finely grated rind of ½ lemon
60ml/4 tbsp raisins
about 1 litre/1¾ pints/4 cups
  sunflower oil, for frying

For sprinkling
60ml/4 tbsp icing (confectioners')
  sugar

12 small squares of baking
  parchment

1 Sift the flour together with the yeast, caster sugar and salt into a bowl. Add the milk, lemon rind and raisins, and mix until combined.

2 Heat the oil in a large, deep pan to 170°C/340°F.

3 Using an ice-cream scoop or two tablespoons, form a ball of batter, and drop it gently into the hot oil. Repeat with the remaining batter, cooking the oliebollen in batches of 3, for 30–60 seconds on each side, or until golden brown all over. Remove the doughnuts from the oil with a slotted spoon and drain on kitchen paper.

4 While still slightly warm, sprinkle the oliebollen with icing sugar to coat them all over.

COOK'S **TIP**
In Holland, oliebollen are a seasonal treat, traditionally cooked and eaten during New Year celebrations.

VARIATIONS
• The raisins are traditional and impart some extra sweetness and varation of texture, however, these can be omitted, if you prefer.
• Add some ground cinnamon to the icing sugar for dusting, for a stronger flavour combination. This is a particularly nice addition when serving as a festive treat.

Energy 293kcal/1228kJ; Protein 4.1g; Carbohydrate 39.1g, of which sugars 18.5g; Fat 14.4g, of which saturates 3.7g; Cholesterol 15mg; Calcium 53mg; Fibre 0.1g; Sodium 151mg.

Loukoumades

These delicious deep-fried treats are from Greece, where they are enjoyed soaked with a lovely honey syrup. The batter is dropped directly into hot oil, so they are not perfectly shaped. These are known as lokma in Turkey, and are sometimes sprinkled with sesame seeds.

Makes | 12

300g/11oz/2¾ cups strong white
 bread flour, plus extra for dusting
7g/¼oz/1½ tsp easy-blend
 (rapid-rise) dried yeast
15ml/1 tbsp caster (superfine) sugar
a pinch of salt
450ml/¾ pint/scant 2 cups full-fat
 (whole) milk, lukewarm
about 1 litre/1¾pints/4 cups
 sunflower oil, for frying

For the honey syrup
100ml/3½fl oz/scant ½ cup
 clear honey
juice of ½ lemon
2.5ml/½ tsp ground cinnamon

1 Sift the flour together with the yeast, sugar and salt into a bowl. Add the milk and mix until combined.

2 Heat the oil in a large, deep pan to 170°C/340°F.

3 Using an ice cream scoop or two tablespoons, form a ball of batter and drop it gently into the hot oil. Repeat with the remaining batter, cooking them in batches of 3 for 30–60 seconds on each side, or until golden brown all over. Remove the loukoumades from the hot oil with a slotted spoon, and drain on kitchen paper.

4 For the syrup, mix the honey with the lemon juice and cinnamon in a small bowl.

5 Drizzle the honey syrup over the loukoumades, while they are still slightly warm.

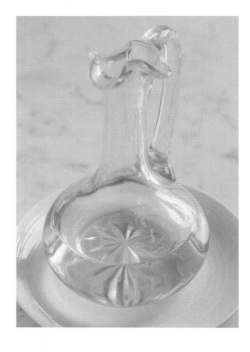

COOK'S **TIP**
Freshly fried loukoumades make a sumptuous and unusual dessert served with Greek yogurt and roughly chopped pistachios.

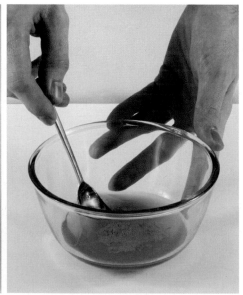

Energy 283kcal/1189kJ; Protein 4g; Carbohydrate 36.8g, of which sugars 16.2g; Fat 14.4g, of which saturates 3.7g; Cholesterol 15mg; Calcium 49mg; Fibre 0g; Sodium 149mg.

Koeksisters

These South African delights are best served cold the next day, once the sugar syrup has had a chance to harden and the dough has turned slightly chewy. The outer crunch is achieved by dunking the piping hot koeksisters into ice-cold syrup. You can make the syrup the day before, and keep it in the refrigerator overnight.

Makes | 12

300g/11oz/2¾ cups plain
   (all-purpose) flour, plus extra
   for dusting
15ml/1 tbsp baking powder
a pinch of salt
30g/1¼oz/2½ tbsp butter, cubed
   and chilled
150ml/¼ pint/⅔ cup full-fat
   (whole) milk
about 1 litre/1¾ pints/4 cups
   sunflower oil, for frying

For the syrup

500g/1¼lb/scant 4½ cups caster
   (superfine) sugar
250ml/8fl oz/1 cup water
juice of 1 lemon
2.5ml/½ tsp ground cinnamon
1.5ml/¼ tsp ground ginger

12 small squares of baking
   parchment

1 Start by making the syrup. Place the sugar, water, lemon juice, cinnamon and ginger in a pan and stir over a low heat until the sugar has dissolved, then bring to a rolling boil for 2 minutes. Remove from the heat, pour the syrup into a heatproof bowl, and leave to cool to room temperature. Refrigerate for at least 1 hour, but preferably overnight.

2 For the koeksisters, sift the flour together with the baking powder and salt into a bowl. Add the butter and rub in until slightly crumbly.

3 Add the milk and knead the mixture for 5 minutes, then shape into a ball. Place in a lightly oiled bowl, cover with clear film (plastic wrap) and leave to stand at room temperature for 1 hour.

4 Roll out the dough on a lightly floured work surface to a rectangle 10cm x 36cm/4in x 14½in, roughly 5mm/¼in thick. Using a sharp knife, cut the dough into 36 strips of 10cm x 1cm/4in x ½in.

5 For each koeksister, take 3 strips of dough and join them together at one end. Braid them together by folding the right strip over the middle strip, followed by the left strip over the last braided strip and so on, until the strips are braided along the whole length. Place each braid on to a baking parchment square.

6 Heat the oil in a large, deep pan to 170°C/340°F. Gently lift the dough braids using the edges of the baking parchment, without disturbing the braids, and slide each one (minus the baking parchment) into the hot oil in batches of 3. Cook them for 30–60 seconds on each side, or until golden brown all over.

7 Remove the braids from the oil with a slotted spoon and drain on kitchen paper. Plunge the braids into the ice-cold syrup while they are still hot, to coat the braids all over. Allow the syrup to set and harden.

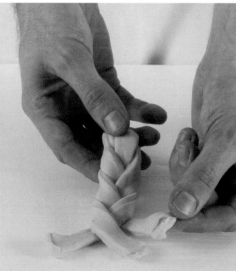
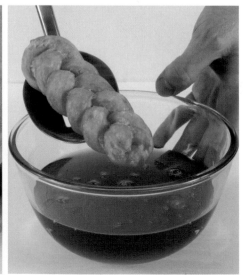

Energy 330kcal/1397kJ; Protein 2.7g; Carbohydrate 63g, of which sugars 49.9g; Fat 9.3g, of which saturates 2.4g; Cholesterol 10mg; Calcium 49mg; Fibre 0g; Sodium 97mg.

MODERN TWISTS

This chapter takes the traditional doughnut and transforms it into wonderful contemporary creations. I have adapted some of my favourite cakes into delicious doughnuts, and developed new ideas from savoury spiced bites to a giant cake, as well as a sumptuously comforting doughnut and butter pudding.

Crème brûlée doughnuts

The classic outer crunch of the crème brûlée is recreated on the tops of these baked yeast doughnuts, which are filled with a silky smooth egg custard. If you do not have a chef's blow torch, you can place the doughnuts under the grill (broiler) to caramelize the sugar instead.

Makes | 12

225g/8oz/2 cups strong white bread
   flour, plus extra for dusting
7g/¼oz/1½ tsp easy-blend
   (rapid-rise) dried yeast
15ml/1 tbsp caster (superfine) sugar
a pinch of salt
65g/2½oz/5 tbsp butter, cubed
   and chilled
1 egg, beaten
120ml/4fl oz/½ cup full-fat (whole)
   milk, lukewarm
about 1 litre/1¾ pints/4 cups
   sunflower oil, for frying

For the crème brûlée filling
250ml/8fl oz/1 cup double
   (heavy) cream
seeds of 1 vanilla pod (bean)
3 egg yolks
50g/2oz/¼ cup caster
   (superfine) sugar

For finishing
115g/4oz/generous ½ cup granulated
   (white) sugar

12 small squares of baking
   parchment

1 First, make the filling. Place the cream and vanilla seeds in a pan, bring to the boil, then remove from the heat. Beat the egg yolks and sugar together in a heatproof bowl until light and fluffy. Gradually pour the hot cream over the egg mixture, stirring constantly until the mixture thickens slightly. Cover the surface with clear film (plastic wrap) and leave to cool. Chill in the refrigerator for at least 1 hour, or until thickened.

2 Meanwhile, sift the flour together with the yeast, caster sugar and salt into a bowl. Add the butter and rub into the flour mixture using your fingertips. Add the egg and milk, and knead the mixture until it all comes together.

3 Turn out the dough on to a lightly floured work surface and knead for 10 minutes, or until silky smooth. Roll into a ball and place back into the bowl, cover with clear film and leave to rest in a warm place for about 1 hour, or until doubled in size.

4 Cut the dough into 12 even pieces and roll into smooth round balls, placing each one on to a baking parchment square.

5 Cover loosely with clear film and leave to stand in a warm place for 30 minutes, until slightly risen.

6 Heat the oil in a large, deep pan to 170°C/340°F. Gently lift the doughnuts using the edges of the baking parchment, without disturbing the doughnuts, and slide each one (minus the baking parchment) into the hot oil, in batches of 3. Cook them for 30–60 seconds on each side, or until golden brown all over. Remove the doughnuts with a slotted spoon, and drain on kitchen paper.

7 While the doughnuts are still warm, poke the handle of a teaspoon into the side of each doughnut, moving the handle around inside the doughnut in a circular motion to make room for the filling. Leave to cool completely.

8 Fill a piping (pastry) bag with the thickened crème brûlée filling and squeeze a small amount into each doughnut. To finish, dip the tops of the doughnuts in the granulated sugar and then use a chef's blow torch to melt the sugar, until golden. Refrigerate them until you are ready to serve.

Energy 338kcal/1412kJ; Protein 3.6g; Carbohydrate 34.1g, of which sugars 21g; Fat 21.7g, of which saturates 9.7g; Cholesterol 89mg; Calcium 51mg; Fibre 0g; Sodium 102mg.

Buttermilk cream doughnuts

Rich and satisfying, buttermilk has become one of my favourite ingredients to use in baking as it creates a velvety texture, and this is especially true with these doughnuts. The addition of raspberries marries perfectly with the buttermilk. Serve with a side of fresh raspberries to cut the sweetness.

Makes | 12

225g/8oz/2 cups strong white bread flour, plus extra for dusting
7g/¼oz/1½ tsp easy-blend (rapid-rise) dried yeast
15ml/1 tbsp caster (superfine) sugar
a pinch of salt
65g/2½oz/5 tbsp butter, cubed and chilled
1 egg, beaten
60ml/4 tbsp full-fat (whole) milk, lukewarm
60ml/4 tbsp buttermilk

For the filling
60ml/4 tbsp raspberry jam

For the glaze
300g/11oz/2¾ cups icing (confectioners') sugar
3 raspberries
30ml/2 tbsp buttermilk

12 small squares of baking parchment

1 Sift the flour together with the yeast, sugar and salt into a bowl. Add the butter and rub into the flour mixture using your fingertips. Add the egg, milk and buttermilk, and knead the mixture until it all comes together.

2 Turn out the dough on to a lightly floured work surface and knead for 10 minutes, or until silky smooth. Roll into a ball and place back into the bowl, cover with clear film (plastic wrap) and leave to rest in a warm place for about 1 hour, or until doubled in size.

3 Cut the dough into 12 even pieces and roll into smooth round balls, placing each one on to a baking parchment square. Cover loosely with clear film, and leave to stand in a warm place for 30 minutes, or until slightly risen.

4 Heat the oil in a large, deep pan to 170°C/340°F.

5 Gently lift the doughnuts using the edges of the baking parchment, without disturbing the doughnuts, and slide each one (minus the baking parchment) into the hot oil in batches of 3. Cook them for 30–60 seconds on each side or until golden brown all over. Remove the doughnuts from the oil with a slotted spoon, and drain on kitchen paper.

6 While the doughnuts are still warm, poke the handle of a teaspoon into the side of each doughnut, moving the handle around inside the doughnut in a circular motion to make room for the filling.

7 For the filling, place the raspberry jam into a piping (pastry) bag and pipe a little jam into each doughnut.

8 To make the glaze, blitz the icing sugar together with the raspberries and buttermilk in a food processor. Dunk the doughnuts in the glaze, then place them on to a cooling rack until set.

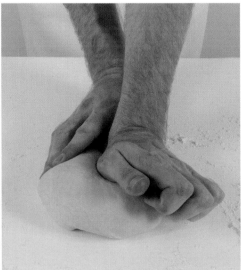

Energy 280kcal/1181kJ; Protein 2.9g; Carbohydrate 49.4g, of which sugars 36.3g; Fat 9.2g, of which saturates 2.4g; Cholesterol 10mg; Calcium 48mg; Fibre 0g; Sodium 101mg.

Baked marbled doughnuts

These marbled doughnuts are a fun addition to this book and aren't a typical doughnut you would find in a bakery, but I'm such a huge fan of marbled cakes that I had to create a doughnut version. Drizzled with a glossy chocolate glaze, they are pretty and easy to make too.

Makes | 12

non-stick baking oil or melted
   butter, for greasing
100g/3¾oz/scant ½ cup
   butter, softened
150g/5oz/¾ cup caster
   (superfine) sugar
5ml/1 tsp vanilla extract
2 eggs
275g/10oz/2½ cups plain
   (all-purpose) flour
10ml/2 tsp baking powder
a pinch of salt
150ml/¼ pint/⅔ cup full-fat
   (whole) milk, plus an extra
   15ml/1 tbsp
25g/1oz/¼ cup unsweetened
   cocoa powder

For the chocolate glaze
100g/3¾oz dark (bittersweet)
   chocolate, broken into pieces
100ml/3½fl oz/scant ½ cup double
   (heavy) cream
30ml/2 tbsp golden (light corn) syrup

1 Preheat the oven to 180°C/350°F/ Gas 4. Spray a 12-cup doughnut baking tin (pan) with non-stick baking oil, or brush with melted butter.

2 Place the softened butter, sugar and vanilla extract in a bowl, and whisk together until light and creamy. Add the eggs, one at a time, whisking to make sure the first one is fully incorporated before adding the second.

3 Sift the flour, baking powder and salt into the mixture, and fold in. Add the 150ml/¼ pint/⅔ cup milk, and mix just until it all comes together. Divide the batter in half, placing one portion of the batter into a separate bowl. Add the cocoa powder to one of the bowls along with the extra 15ml/1 tbsp milk, and fold in until fully incorporated.

4 Divide the vanilla batter evenly between the cups in the prepared baking tin, then top with the cocoa batter, dividing it evenly too.

5 Using a small fork, twist and turn the batters into each other, to form a marbled effect. Place the tin in the middle of the oven and bake for 15 minutes, until golden brown. Leave to stand in the tin for 5 minutes, then transfer the doughnuts to a wire rack to cool completely.

6 To make the chocolate glaze, melt the chocolate, cream and syrup together in a non-stick pan over a medium heat, stirring until smooth and glossy. Drizzle the glaze over the doughnuts using a spoon, and allow to set before serving.

Energy 307kcal/1282kJ; Protein 4.5g; Carbohydrate 34.3g, of which sugars 16.5g; Fat 17.8g, of which saturates 10.5g; Cholesterol 74mg; Calcium 54mg; Fibre 1.6g; Sodium 95mg.

Baked red velvet doughnuts

These beautiful red velvet doughnuts bring two classic tastes of America together. The indulgent cream cheese glaze works deliciously with the sweet doughnuts, and, because the doughnuts are baked rather than fried, they are reminiscent of traditional red velvet cakes.

Makes | 12

non-stick baking oil or melted butter,
  for greasing and brushing
100g/3¾oz/scant ½ cup
  butter, softened
150g/5oz/¾ cup caster
  (superfine) sugar
5ml/1 tsp vanilla extract
2 eggs
275g/10oz/2½ cups plain
  (all-purpose) flour
10ml/2 tsp baking powder
a pinch of salt
100ml/3½fl oz/scant ½ cup full-fat
  (whole) milk
50ml/2fl oz/¼ cup buttermilk
50g/2oz/½ cup unsweetened
  cocoa powder
7.5ml/1½ tsp red food
  colouring paste

For the cream cheese glaze
150g/5oz/1¼ cups icing
  (confectioners') sugar
50g/2oz/¼ cup cream cheese
50ml/2fl oz/¼ cup buttermilk

1 Preheat the oven to 180°C/350°F/ Gas 4. Spray a 12-cup doughnut baking tin (pan) with non-stick baking oil, or brush with melted butter.

2 Place the softened butter, caster sugar and vanilla extract in a bowl and whisk together until light and creamy. Add the eggs, one at a time, whisking to make sure the first one is fully incorporated before adding the second.

3 Sift the flour, baking powder and salt into the mixture and fold in. Add the milk and buttermilk, and mix just until it all comes together. Mix the cocoa powder with the red food colouring paste and fold this into the batter until combined.

4 Transfer the mixture to a piping (pastry) bag fitted with a round nozzle, then pipe the mixture into the prepared baking tin, dividing it evenly between the cups. Piping the mixture makes it easier to create neat circles, but you can spoon the mixture into the tin, if you prefer.

5 Place the tin in the middle of the oven and bake for 15 minutes, or until lightly golden. Leave to stand for 5 minutes before removing the doughnuts from the tin, then transfer them to a wire rack.

6 For the glaze, whisk the icing sugar with the cream cheese and buttermilk, until smooth. Spoon the glaze over the tops of the doughnuts, while they are still slightly warm, allowing the glaze to run down the sides a little, if you like. Allow to set.

Energy 294kcal/1235kJ; Protein 5g; Carbohydrate 45.3g, of which sugars 27.2g; Fat 11.5g, of which saturates 6.7g; Cholesterol 62mg; Calcium 73mg; Fibre 1.6g; Sodium 128mg.

Baked banana bread doughnuts

Banana bread has to be one of my favourite things, so I thought I would recreate it in delicious banana bread doughnuts. This is a good way of using up any overripe bananas you may have, as they impart sweet and fruity flavours to these light and fluffy baked doughnuts.

Makes | 12

non-stick baking oil or melted
  butter, for greasing
100g/3¾oz/scant ½ cup
  butter, softened
150g/5oz/¾ cup caster
  (superfine) sugar
5ml/1 tsp vanilla extract
2 eggs
275g/10oz/2½ cups plain
  (all-purpose) flour
10ml/2 tsp baking powder
a pinch of salt
50ml/2fl oz/¼ cup full-fat (whole) milk
3 ripe bananas
icing (confectioners') sugar,
  for sprinkling

1 Preheat the oven to 180°C/350°F/Gas 4. Spray a 12-cup doughnut baking tin (pan) with non-stick baking oil, or brush with melted butter.

2 Place the softened butter, caster sugar and vanilla extract in a bowl, and whisk together until light and creamy. Add the eggs, one at a time, whisking to make sure the first one is fully incorporated before adding the second.

3 Sift the flour, baking powder and salt into the mixture, and fold in. Add the milk, and mix just until it all comes together. Peel and mash the bananas with a fork and then fold into the batter until fully incorporated.

4 Transfer the mixture to a piping (pastry) bag fitted with a round nozzle, then pipe the mixture into the prepared baking tin, dividing it evenly between the cups. Piping the mixture makes it easier to create neat circles, but you can spoon the mixture into the tin, if you prefer.

5 Place the tin in the middle of the oven and bake for 15 minutes, or until golden brown. Leave to stand for 5 minutes before removing them from the tin.

6 Lightly sprinkle with icing sugar, while they are still slightly warm.

VARIATION

For a new dimension, add 5ml/1 tsp ground ginger and 5ml/1 tsp ground cinnamon to the mixture.

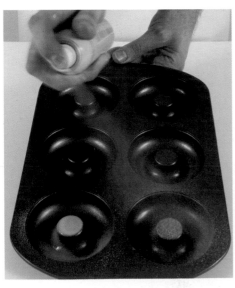

Energy 153kcal/640kJ; Protein 1.8g; Carbohydrate 19.1g, of which sugars 18.5g; Fat 8.2g, of which saturates 4.8g; Cholesterol 57mg; Calcium 17mg; Fibre 0.4g; Sodium 67mg.

Black Forest doughnuts

Gorgeous, juicy and plump cherries line the filling of these cream-filled doughnuts, with the addition of extra cherry jam and topped with icing sugar. Black Forest gâteau has never tasted so good! You can either serve each doughnut on its own or pile 2 or 3 on top of each other for the layered effect of the classic gâteau.

Makes | 12

non-stick baking oil or melted
   butter, for greasing
100g/3¾oz/scant ½ cup
   butter, softened
150g/5oz/¾ cup caster
   (superfine) sugar
5ml/1 tsp vanilla extract
2 eggs
275g/10oz/2½ cups plain
   (all-purpose) flour
10ml/2 tsp baking powder
a pinch of salt
30g/1¼oz/generous ¼ cup
   unsweetened cocoa powder
150ml/¼ pint/⅔ cup full-fat
   (whole) milk

For the filling
100g/3¾oz cherry jam
150ml/¼ pint/⅔ cup double (heavy)
   cream, whipped to stiff peaks

For the topping
100g/3¾oz dark (bittersweet)
   chocolate, broken into pieces
150ml/¼ pint/⅔ cup double
   (heavy) cream
30ml/2 tbsp golden
   (light corn) syrup

1 Preheat the oven to 180°C/350°F/Gas 4. Spray a 12-cup doughnut baking tin (pan) with non-stick baking oil, or brush with melted butter.

2 Place the softened butter, caster sugar and vanilla extract in a bowl and whisk together until light and creamy. Add the eggs, one at a time, whisking to make sure the first one is fully incorporated before adding the second.

3 Sift the flour, baking powder, salt and cocoa powder into the mixture, and fold in. Add the milk and mix just until it all comes together.

4 Transfer the mixture to a piping (pastry) bag fitted with a round nozzle, then pipe the mixture into the prepared baking tin, dividing it evenly between the cups. Piping the mixture makes it easier to create neat circles, but you can spoon the mixture into the tin, if you prefer.

5 Place the tin in the middle of the oven and bake for 15 minutes, until lightly browned. Leave to stand for 5 minutes before removing the doughnuts from the tin. Transfer to a wire rack to cool.

6 Cut each doughnut in half, like a bagel. Spread one half with cherry jam, then top with a layer of whipped cream. Top with the other half of the doughnut, being careful not to squash out the filling. Repeat with the remaining doughnuts.

7 For the chocolate topping, melt the chocolate, cream and syrup in a pan, stirring until smooth and glossy. Spread the chocolate glaze on to the tops of the doughnuts. Serve them in a stack, if you like, when the topping is dry.

Energy 401kcal/1677kJ; Protein 4g; Carbohydrate 45.2g, of which sugars 27.4g; Fat 23.9g, of which saturates 14.8g; Cholesterol 54mg; Calcium 71mg; Fibre 1.6g; Sodium 98mg.

Coconut doughnuts

A light coating of desiccated coconut creates a beautiful and unusual finish here. With coconut milk in both the dough and glaze, these delightful morsels celebrate the exotic coconut in its entirety, and with a subtle hint of zesty lime in the glaze, you will be transported to a tropical island in one bite.

Makes | 12

225g/8oz/2 cups strong white bread
 flour, plus extra for dusting
7g/¼oz/1½ tsp easy-blend
 (rapid-rise) dried yeast
15ml/1 tbsp caster (superfine) sugar
a pinch of salt
65g/2½oz/5 tbsp butter, cubed
 and chilled
1 egg, beaten
60ml/4 tbsp full-fat (whole) milk
60ml/4 tbsp coconut milk
about 1 litre/1¾ pints/4 cups
 sunflower oil, for frying

For the glaze
300g/11oz/2¾ cups icing
 (confectioners') sugar
120ml/4fl oz/½ cup coconut milk
finely grated rind of 1 lime

For sprinkling
150g/5oz desiccated (dry
 unsweetened shredded) coconut

12 small squares of baking
 parchment

1 Sift the flour together with the yeast, caster sugar and salt into a mixing bowl. Add the butter to the bowl and rub it into the flour mixture using your fingertips. Add the beaten egg, milk and coconut milk, and then knead the mixture until it all comes together.

2 Turn out the dough on to a lightly floured work surface and knead for 10 minutes, or until silky smooth. Roll into a ball and place back into the bowl, cover with clear film (plastic wrap) and leave to rest in a warm place for about 1 hour or until doubled in size.

3 Cut the dough into 12 even pieces and roll into smooth round balls, placing each one on to a baking parchment square. Cover loosely with clear film and leave to stand in a warm place for 30 minutes, or until slightly risen.

4 Heat the oil in a large, deep pan to 170°C/340°F.

5 Gently lift the doughnuts using the edges of the baking parchment, without disturbing the doughnuts, and slide each one (minus the baking parchment) into the hot oil in batches of 3. Cook them for 30–60 seconds on each side, or until golden brown all over. Remove the doughnuts from the oil with a slotted spoon and drain on kitchen paper.

6 For the glaze, mix the icing sugar with the coconut milk and lime rind to a smooth paste. Brush the glaze on to the tops of the doughnuts, while they are still slightly warm, then sprinkle with desiccated coconut. Leave to set.

Energy 341kcal/1433kJ; Protein 3.4g; Carbohydrate 46.8g, of which sugars 33.7g; Fat 17g, of which saturates 9.1g; Cholesterol 10mg; Calcium 44mg; Fibre 2.3g; Sodium 110mg.

Peanut butter and jelly doughnuts

Who does not love the classic peanut butter and jelly combination? Adored by children and adults alike, it's that sweet and salty mix that hits home every time. In this recipe, 'jelly' refers to the preserve that is also known as 'jam', rather than the gelatine-based dessert. Look for raspberry jam in the UK or raspberry jelly in the USA.

Makes | 12

225g/8oz/2 cups strong white bread flour, plus extra for dusting
7g/¼oz/1½ tsp easy-blend (rapid-rise) dried yeast
15ml/1 tbsp caster (superfine) sugar
a pinch of salt
65g/2½oz/5 tbsp butter, cubed and chilled
1 egg, beaten
120ml/4fl oz/½ cup full-fat (whole) milk, lukewarm
about 1 litre/1¾ pints/4 cups sunflower oil, for frying

For the filling
65g/2½oz raspberry jam or jelly
65g/2½oz peanut butter

For coating
115g/4oz/generous ½ cup granulated (white) sugar

12 small squares of baking parchment

1 Sift the flour together with the yeast, sugar and salt into a bowl. Add the butter and rub into the flour mixture using your fingertips. Add the egg and milk, and knead the mixture until it all comes together.

2 Turn out the dough on to a lightly floured work surface and knead for 10 minutes, or until silky smooth. Roll into a ball and place in a clean, lightly greased bowl. Cover with clear film (plastic wrap) and leave to rest in a warm place for about 1 hour, or until doubled in size.

3 Cut the dough into 12 even pieces and roll them into smooth round balls, placing each one on to a baking parchment square. Cover the balls loosely with clear film, and leave to stand in a warm place for 30 minutes, until slightly risen.

4 Heat the oil in a large, deep pan to 170°C/340°F.

5 Gently lift the doughnuts using the edges of the baking parchment, without disturbing the doughnuts, and slide each one (minus the baking parchment) into the hot oil in batches of 3. Cook them for 30–60 seconds on each side, or until golden brown all over. Remove the doughnuts from the oil with a slotted spoon and drain on kitchen paper.

6 While the doughnuts are still warm, poke the handle of a teaspoon into the side of each doughnut, moving the handle around inside the doughnut in a circular motion to make room for the filling.

7 Fill a piping (pastry) bag with the jam and squeeze a small amount into each doughnut. Fill another piping bag with the peanut butter and repeat, so that each doughnut contains both jam and peanut butter. Place the sugar for coating on a plate, and toss the doughnuts in the sugar to coat them completely.

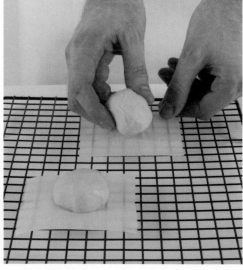

Energy 250kcal/1050kJ; Protein 3.8g; Carbohydrate 33.8g, of which sugars 20.4g; Fat 12g, of which saturates 3.1g; Cholesterol 10mg; Calcium 37mg; Fibre 0g; Sodium 115mg.

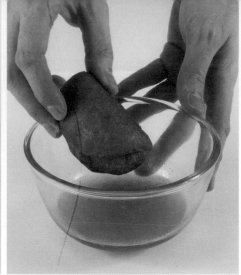

Pistachio pockets

Pistachios are a great comfort food and they bring their taste, texture and colour to many cakes and bakes. These doughnuts showcase the properties of pistachos perfectly – with a mouthwatering pistachio butter at the centre of each crisp and sweet doughnut pocket.

Makes | 12

225g/8oz/2 cups strong white bread
  flour, plus extra for dusting
7g/¼oz/1½ tsp easy-blend
  (rapid-rise) dried yeast
15ml/1 tbsp caster (superfine) sugar
a pinch of salt
65g/2½oz/5 tbsp butter, cubed
  and chilled
1 egg, beaten
120ml/4fl oz/½ cup full-fat (whole)
  milk, lukewarm
about 1 litre/1¾ pints/4 cups
  sunflower oil, for frying

For the pistachio paste
200g/7oz/1¾ cups ground pistachios
100g/3¾oz/generous ½ cup caster
  (superfine) sugar
30ml/2 tbsp clear honey

For the syrup
100g/3¾oz/scant ½ cup clear honey
50ml/2fl oz/¼ cup lemon juice
5ml/1 tsp ground cinnamon

12 squares of baking parchment

1 Sift the flour together with the yeast, sugar and salt into a bowl. Add the butter, and rub into the flour mixture using your fingertips. Add the egg and milk, and knead the mixture until it all comes together.

2 Turn out the dough on to a lightly floured work surface and knead for 10 minutes, or until silky smooth. Roll into a ball and place back into the bowl, cover with clear film (plastic wrap) and leave to rest in a warm place for about 1 hour, or until doubled in size.

3 Make the pistachio paste by mixing the ground pistachios with the sugar and honey to form a smooth paste. Set aside. Roll out the dough on a lightly floured work surface until it is roughly 1cm/½in thick, then using a 9cm/3½in plain round cookie cutter, cut out 12 rounds.

4 Divide the pistachio paste between the rounds, then fold the dough over and press the edges together to seal. Place each pocket on a square of baking parchment, cover loosely with clear film and leave to stand in a warm place for 30 minutes, or until slightly risen.

5 Heat the oil in a large, deep pan to 170°C/340°F. Gently lift the pistachio pockets using the edges of the baking parchment, without disturbing the doughnuts, and slide each one (minus the baking parchment) into the hot oil in batches of 3. Cook them for 30–60 seconds on each side, or until golden brown all over. Remove the doughnuts from the oil with a slotted spoon and drain on kitchen paper.

6 For the syrup, mix the honey with the lemon juice and cinnamon. Dunk the pistachio pockets into the syrup, while still slightly warm, and place on a wire rack to set.

Energy 329kcal/1380kJ; Protein 5.6g; Carbohydrate 37.7g, of which sugars 24.2g; Fat 18.4g, of which saturates 3.6g; Cholesterol 10mg; Calcium 58mg; Fibre 1.4g; Sodium 184mg.

Polenta honey doughnuts

Grainy and moist polenta is used to create doughnuts with an unusual texture in this recipe. Combined with a simple honey filling, and rolled in plenty of icing sugar, this will be a favourite recipe if you have a sweet tooth. Polenta is a traditonal grain in Italy, but here it provides an unique twist on a classic.

Makes | 12

150g/5oz/1¼ cups strong white
  bread flour
7g/¼oz/1½ tsp easy-blend
  (rapid-rise) dried yeast
15ml/1 tbsp caster (superfine) sugar
a pinch of salt
75g/3oz/scant ¾ cup polenta
65g/2½oz/5 tbsp butter, cubed
  and chilled
120ml/4fl oz/½ cup full-fat
  (whole) milk, lukewarm
about 1 litre/1¾ pints/4 cups
  sunflower oil, for frying

For the filling
150ml/¼ pint/generous ½ cup
  clear honey

For coating
115g/4oz/1 cup icing
  (confectioners') sugar

12 small squares of baking
  parchment

1 Sift the flour together with the yeast, sugar and salt into a bowl. Add the polenta and butter, and rub in until slightly crumbly. Add the milk and knead the mixture until it all comes together.

2 Turn out the dough on to a lightly floured work surface and knead for 10 minutes. Roll into a ball and place back into the bowl, cover with clear film (plastic wrap) and leave to rest in a warm place for about 1 hour, or until doubled in size.

3 Cut the dough into 12 even pieces and roll into smooth round balls, placing each one on to a baking parchment square. Cover loosely with clear film and leave to stand in a warm place for 30 minutes, until slightly risen.

4 Heat the oil in a large, deep pan to 170ºC/340ºF. Gently lift the doughnuts using the edges of the baking parchment, without disturbing the doughnuts, and slide each one (minus the baking parchment) into the hot oil in batches of 3. Cook them for 30–60 seconds on each side, or until golden brown all over.

5 Remove the doughnuts from the oil with a slotted spoon and drain on kitchen paper. While the doughnuts are still warm, poke the handle of a small teaspoon into the side of each doughnut, moving the handle around inside the doughnut to make room for the filling.

6 Place the honey into a piping (pastry) bag, and pipe a small amount into each doughnut.

7 Place the icing sugar for coating on a plate, and roll the doughnuts in it, to cover completely.

Energy 219kcal/922kJ; Protein 2.3g; Carbohydrate 36.6g, of which sugars 25.1g; Fat 8.1g, of which saturates 2.1g; Cholesterol 9mg; Calcium 31mg; Fibre 0g; Sodium 85mg.

Orange ricotta doughnuts

These flavourful orange and ricotta doughnuts are zingy and fresh. I like to make them on a Saturday night, so that they are ready to be enjoyed for a lazy Sunday breakfast. If you do make them in advance, store them in the refrigerator, until you are ready to serve them.

Makes | 12

225g/8oz/2 cups strong
 white bread flour, plus extra
 for dusting
7g/¼oz/1½ tsp easy-blend
 (rapid-rise) dried yeast
15ml/1 tbsp caster (superfine) sugar
a pinch of salt
finely grated rind of ½ orange
50g/2oz/¼ cup butter, cubed
 and chilled
1 egg, beaten
120ml/4fl oz/½ cup full-fat (whole)
 milk, lukewarm
150g/5oz/⅔ cup ricotta cheese
about 1 litre/1¾ pints/4 cups
 sunflower oil, for frying

For the filling
150g/5oz/⅔ cup ricotta
30ml/2 tbsp orange juice

For coating
115g/4oz/generous ½ cup granulated
 (white) sugar
finely grated rind of ½ orange

12 small squares of baking
 parchment

1 Sift the flour together with the yeast, sugar and salt into a bowl. Stir in the orange rind. Add the butter and rub into the flour mixture using your fingertips. Add the egg, milk and ricotta, and knead the mixture until it all comes together.

2 Turn out the dough on to a lightly floured work surface and knead for 10 minutes, or until silky smooth. Roll into a ball and place back into the bowl, cover with clear film (plastic wrap) and leave to rest in a warm place for about 1 hour, or until doubled in size.

3 Cut the dough into 12 even pieces and roll into smooth round balls, placing each one on to a baking parchment square. Cover loosely with clear film and leave to stand in a warm place for 30 minutes, or until slightly risen.

4 Heat the oil in a large, deep pan to 170°C/340°F. Gently lift the doughnuts using the edges of the baking parchment, without disturbing the doughnuts, and slide each one (minus the baking parchment) into the hot oil in batches of 3. Cook them for 30–60 seconds on each side, or until golden brown all over.

5 Remove the doughnuts from the oil with a slotted spoon and drain on kitchen paper.

6 While the doughnuts are still warm, poke the handle of a teaspoon into the side of each doughnut, moving the handle around inside the doughnut in a circular motion to make room for the filling.

7 For the filling, mix the ricotta with the orange juice. Fill a piping (pastry) bag with the orange ricotta, and squeeze a small amount into each doughnut. Mix the sugar and orange rind for coating together on a plate. Toss the doughnuts in it to coat them completely.

COOK'S **TIP**
These are nice served for brunch with some Greek (US strained plain) yogurt on the side, for dipping. For an extra-tasty accompaniment, mix 20ml/4 tsp orange juice into 100ml/3½fl oz/ scant ½ cup Greek yogurt.

Energy 240kcal/1007kJ; Protein 4.9g; Carbohydrate 30.1g, of which sugars 17g; Fat 11.9g, of which saturates 4.1g; Cholesterol 22mg; Calcium 94mg; Fibre 0g; Sodium 120mg.

Oatmeal doughnuts

These oatmeal rings are a slightly healthier alternative to the usual doughnut. Treat them like you would a bagel – they are delicious sliced in half, toasted and spread with a generous serving of low-fat cream cheese. Perfect for brunch. Use honey instead of syrup to coat them, if you prefer.

Makes | 12

225g/8oz/2 cups strong white bread flour, plus extra for dusting
75g/3oz /scant ¼ cup oatmeal
7g/¼oz/1½ tsp easy-blend (rapid-rise) dried yeast
15ml/1 tbsp caster (superfine) sugar
a pinch of salt
65g/2½oz/5 tbsp butter, cubed and chilled
1 egg, beaten
120ml/4fl oz/½ cup full-fat (whole) milk, lukewarm
about 1 litre/1¾ pints/4 cups sunflower oil, for frying

For the topping
100g/3¾oz/generous ¼ cup golden (light corn) syrup
50g/2oz/½ cup rolled oats

1 Sift the flour together with the oatmeal, yeast, sugar and salt into a bowl. Add the butter, and rub into the flour mixture using your fingertips. Add the egg and milk, and knead the mixture until it all comes together.

2 Turn out the dough on to a lightly floured work surface and knead for 10 minutes, or until silky smooth. Roll into a ball and place back into the bowl, cover with clear film (plastic wrap) and leave to rest in a warm place for about 1 hour, or until doubled in size.

3 Roll out the dough on a lightly floured work surface until it is roughly 1cm/½in thick. Using a doughnut cookie cutter, cut out 12 rings and place each of these on to a baking parchment square. Cover loosely with clear film and leave to stand in a warm place for 30 minutes, until slightly risen.

4 Heat the oil in a large, deep pan to 170°C/340°F.

5 Gently lift the doughnuts using the edges of the baking parchment, without disturbing the doughnuts, and slide each one (minus the baking parchment) into the hot oil in batches of 3. Cook them for 30–60 seconds on each side, or until golden brown all over. Remove the doughnuts from the oil with a slotted spoon, and drain on kitchen paper.

6 For the topping, drizzle a little golden syrup on to each doughnut, while still slightly warm, and brush to coat evenly. Sprinkle with rolled oats.

Energy 207kcal/869kJ; Protein 3g; Carbohydrate 29g, of which sugars 12.9g; Fat 9.6g, of which saturates 2.4g; Cholesterol 10mg; Calcium 35mg; Fibre 0.4g; Sodium 118mg.

Corn and cumin doughnuts

Out of all the doughnuts in this book, these corn and cumin flavoured ones turned out to be my absolute favourite. I think it has to do with the texture of the cornmeal and the subtle spice of the cumin, which is such a gorgeous combination. These are very simple, yet oh so good.

Makes | 12

150g/5oz/1¼ cups strong white
  bread flour
7g/¼oz/1½ tsp easy-blend
  (rapid-rise) dried yeast
a pinch of salt
75g/3oz/scant ¾ cup fine cornmeal
25g/1oz/2 tbsp butter, cubed
  and chilled
1 egg
120ml/4fl oz/½ cup full-fat
  (whole) milk
about 1 litre/1¾ pints/4 cups
  sunflower oil, for frying

For sprinkling
90ml/6 tbsp caster (superfine) sugar
5ml/1 tsp ground cumin

12 small squares of baking
  parchment

1 Sift the flour together with the yeast and salt. Add the cornmeal and butter, and rub in until slightly crumbly. Add the egg and milk, and knead the mixture until it all comes together.

2 Turn out the dough on to a lightly floured work surface and knead for 10 minutes, then shape into a ball. Place in a lightly oiled bowl, cover with clear film (plastic wrap) and leave to stand at room temperature for about 1 hour, or until doubled in size.

3 Cut the dough into 12 even pieces and roll into smooth round balls, placing each one on to a baking parchment square. Cover loosely with clear film and leave to stand in a warm place for 30 minutes, until slightly risen.

VARIATION
For a savoury twist, omit the sugar coating, and accompany with a little chilli jam for dipping.

4 Heat the oil in a large, deep pan to 170°C/340°F. Gently lift the doughnuts using the edges of the baking parchment, without disturbing the doughnuts, and slide each one (minus the baking parchment) into the hot oil in batches of 3. Cook them for 30–60 seconds on each side, or until golden brown all over. Remove the doughnuts from the oil with a slotted spoon and drain on kitchen paper.

5 For sprinkling, mix the sugar and cumin together and sprinkle over the doughnuts while still warm.

Energy 176kcal/741kJ; Protein 2.3g; Carbohydrate 25g, of which sugars 13.4g; Fat 8.2g, of which saturates 2.1g; Cholesterol 9mg; Calcium 34mg; Fibre 0g; Sodium 85mg.

Maple bacon doughnuts

Introducing savoury into sweet is always exciting, especially when the savoury is quite salty. Anyone who has tried fried bacon drizzled with maple syrup will know how good it tastes, and it works really well in these moreish doughnuts. This recipe surprised all my family and friends, and ended up a firm favourite.

Makes | 12

225g/8oz/2 cups strong white bread flour, plus extra for dusting
7g/¼oz/1½ tsp easy-blend (rapid-rise) dried yeast
15ml/1 tbsp caster (superfine) sugar
a pinch of salt
65g/2½oz/5 tbsp butter, cubed and chilled
1 egg, beaten
120ml/4fl oz/½ cup full-fat (whole) milk, lukewarm
about 1 litre/1¾ pints/4 cups sunflower oil, for frying

For the topping
100ml/3½fl oz/scant ½ cup maple syrup
4 streaky (fatty) bacon rashers (strips), fried and finely chopped

12 small squares of baking parchment

1 Sift the flour together with the yeast, caster sugar and salt into a bowl. Add the butter, and rub into the flour mixture using your fingertips. Add the egg and milk, and knead the mixture until it all comes together.

2 Turn out the dough on to a lightly floured work surface and knead for 10 minutes, or until silky smooth. Roll into a ball and place back into the bowl, cover with clear film (plastic wrap) and leave to rest in a warm place for about 1 hour, or until doubled in size.

3 Roll out the dough on a lightly floured work surface until it is roughly 1cm/½in thick, then, using a doughnut cookie cutter, cut out 12 rings and place each of these on to a baking parchment square. Cover loosely with clear film and leave to stand in a warm place for 30 minutes, until slightly risen.

4 Heat the oil in a large, deep pan to 170ºC/340ºF.

5 Gently lift the doughnuts using the edges of the baking parchment, without disturbing the doughnuts, and slide each one (minus the baking parchment) into the hot oil in batches of 3. Cook them for 30–60 seconds on each side, or until golden brown all over. Remove the doughnuts from the oil with a slotted spoon and drain on kitchen paper.

6 For the topping, drizzle the maple syrup over the tops of the doughnuts, while still slightly warm, and brush to coat evenly. Sprinkle with the bacon.

Baked pumpkin doughnuts

These lightly spiced doughnuts are the perfect bite for the autumn months when the days start drawing in and a little burst of comfort food is needed. Serve with a little whipped cream for an extra special sweet treat. You can buy pumpkin purée in cans, or cook some chunks of pumpkin at home and blitz it in a food processor.

Makes │12

non-stick baking oil or melted
   butter, for greasing
100g/3¾oz/scant ½ cup
   butter, softened
150g/5oz/¾ cup caster
   (superfine) sugar
5ml/1 tsp vanilla extract
2 eggs
300g/11oz/2¾ cups plain
   (all-purpose) flour
10ml/2 tsp baking powder
a pinch of salt
100ml/3½fl oz/scant ½ cup full-fat
   (whole) milk
100g/3¾oz canned pumpkin purée

For the topping
65g/2½oz/9 tbsp icing
   (confectioners') sugar
1.5ml/¼ tsp ground cinnamon
a pinch of ground nutmeg

1 Preheat the oven to 180°C/350°F/ Gas 4. Spray a 12-cup doughnut baking tin (pan) with non-stick baking oil, or brush with melted butter.

2 Place the softened butter, sugar and vanilla extract in a bowl, and whisk together until light and creamy. Add the eggs, one at a time, whisking to make sure the first one is fully incorporated before adding the second.

3 Sift the flour, baking powder and salt into the mixture, and fold in. Add the milk, and mix just until it all comes together. Fold in the pumpkin purée.

4 Transfer the mixture to a piping (pastry) bag fitted with a round nozzle, then pipe the mixture into the prepared baking tin, dividing it evenly between the cups. Piping the mixture makes it easier to create neat circles, but you can spoon the mixture into the tin, if you prefer.

5 Place the tin in the middle of the oven and bake for 15 minutes, or until golden brown. Leave to stand for 5 minutes before removing the doughnuts from the tin.

6 For the topping, mix the sugar with the cinnamon and nutmeg, then sprinkle over the doughnuts, while still slightly warm, to coat completely.

Energy 284kcal/1193kJ; Protein 4.1g; Carbohydrate 36.5g, of which sugars 15.8g; Fat 14.6g, of which saturates 3.8g; Cholesterol 16mg; Calcium 55mg; Fibre 0.1g; Sodium 150mg.

Potato doughnuts

A sticky glaze coats these light and fluffy potato doughnuts, which are decorated with elegant white sprinkles. You need only a small amount of mashed potatoes in the dough, so this is a good recipe for using up leftovers. I sometimes make more mashed potatoes than I need for dinner, so that I can make these the next day!

Makes | 12

300g/11oz/2¾ cups strong
  white bread flour, plus extra
  for dusting
7g/¼oz/1½ tsp easy-blend
  (rapid-rise) dried yeast
15ml/1 tbsp caster (superfine) sugar
a pinch of salt
150g/5oz mashed potatoes
40g/1½oz/3 tbsp butter, cubed
  and chilled
1 egg, beaten
120ml/4fl oz/½ cup full-fat (whole)
  milk, lukewarm
melted butter, for greasing
  and brushing

For the glaze
300g/11oz/2¾ cups icing
  (confectioners') sugar
50ml/2fl oz/¼ cup water

For decorating
60ml/4 tbsp white sprinkles

1 Sift the flour together with the yeast, caster sugar and salt into a bowl. Add the mashed potatoes and butter, and rub into the flour mixture using your fingertips. Add the egg and milk, and knead the mixture until it all comes together.

2 Turn out the dough on to a lightly floured work surface and knead for 10 minutes, or until silky smooth. Roll into a ball and place back into the bowl, cover with clear film (plastic wrap) and leave to rest in a warm place for about 1 hour or until doubled in size.

3 Cut the dough into 12 even pieces and roll into smooth round balls, placing each one on to a baking parchment square. Cover loosely with clear film and leave to stand in a warm place for 30 minutes, until slightly risen.

4 Heat the oil in a large, deep pan to 170°C/340°F.

5 Gently lift the doughnuts using the edges of the baking parchment, without disturbing the doughnuts, and slide each one (minus the baking parchment) into the hot oil in batches of 3. Cook them for 30–60 seconds on each side, or until golden brown all over. Remove the doughnuts from the oil with a slotted spoon and drain on kitchen paper.

6 For the glaze, mix the icing sugar with the water in a small bowl until smooth and combined.

7 Spoon the glaze over the doughnuts, while still slightly warm, to coat all over. Cover with sprinkles, then leave to set before serving.

COOK'S **TIP**
You can use a packet of instant mashed potatoes, if you like.

Energy 281kcal/1184kJ; Protein 2.8g; Carbohydrate 46.9g, of which sugars 32.4g; Fat 10.4g, of which saturates 3.2g; Cholesterol 13mg; Calcium 40mg; Fibre 0.2g; Sodium 96mg.

Mozzarella doughnuts

For a delicious melted cheesy centre, try these mozzarella doughnuts, ideal served straight from the pan and dusted lightly with sugar, for a blissful savoury/sweet experience reminiscent of pizza nights. Mini mozzarella balls are the size of large marbles, and are sometimes called mozzarella pearls.

Makes | 12

225g/8oz/2 cups strong white bread flour, plus extra for dusting
7g/¼oz/1½ tsp easy-blend (rapid-rise) dried yeast
15ml/1 tbsp caster (superfine) sugar
a pinch of salt
65g/2½oz/5 tbsp butter, cubed and chilled
1 egg, beaten
120ml/4fl oz/½ cup full-fat (whole) milk, lukewarm
12 mini mozzarella balls
about 1 litre/1¾ pints/4 cups sunflower oil, for frying

For coating
60ml/4 tbsp icing (confectioners') sugar

12 small squares of baking parchment

1 Sift the flour together with the yeast, sugar and salt into a bowl. Add the butter and rub into the flour mixture using your fingertips. Add the egg and milk, and knead the mixture until it all comes together.

2 Turn out the dough on to a lightly floured work surface and knead for 10 minutes, or until silky smooth. Roll into a ball and place back into the bowl, cover with clear film (plastic wrap) and leave to rest in a warm place for about 1 hour, or until doubled in size.

3 Cut the dough into 12 even pieces and roll into smooth round balls, then flatten slightly into rounds. Place a mozzarella ball in the centre of each round, then fold the dough around the mozzarella, pinching the edges together and re-shaping them into balls. Place each one on to a baking parchment square. Cover loosely with clear film and leave to stand in a warm place for 30 minutes, or until slightly risen.

4 Heat the oil in a large, deep pan to 170°C/340°F.

5 Gently lift the doughnuts using the edges of the baking parchment, without disturbing the doughnuts, and slide each one (minus the baking parchment) into the hot oil in batches of 3. Cook them for 30–60 seconds on each side, or until golden brown all over. Remove the doughnuts from the oil with a slotted spoon and drain on kitchen paper.

6 Sprinkle the warm doughnuts with sugar to coat them completely, and serve immediately, while the mozzarella is still melted and gooey in the centre.

VARIATION
For a more savoury finish, omit the sugar coating, and serve with some tomato sauce for dipping.

Energy 217kcal/910kJ; Protein 4.9g; Carbohydrate 24.6g, of which sugars 11.5g; Fat 11.7g, of which saturates 4.1g; Cholesterol 17mg; Calcium 78mg; Fibre 0g; Sodium 144mg.

Doughnut cake

This is a wonderful celebratory doughnut cake, fit for any birthday party, but kids will especially love this one as it's just one huge chocolate-covered doughnut! This cake provides 12 generous slices. The doughnut mould is available to buy online or from baking specialists – it creates one hollow side, which you fill with buttercream.

Makes | 1 cake

non-stick baking oil or melted butter,
  for greasing
100g/3¾oz/scant ½ cup
  butter, softened
150g/5oz/¾ cup caster
  (superfine) sugar
5ml/1 tsp vanilla extract
2 eggs
275g/10oz/2½ cups plain
  (all-purpose) flour
10ml/2 tsp baking powder
a pinch of salt
150ml/¼ pint/⅔ cup full-fat (whole) milk

For the chocolate buttercream
150g/5oz/10 tbsp butter, softened
300g/11oz/2¾ cups icing
  (confectioners') sugar
100ml/3½fl oz/scant ½ cup double
  (heavy) cream
50g/2oz/½ cup unsweetened
  cocoa powder

For the glaze and decoration
100g/3¾oz dark (bittersweet)
  chocolate, broken into pieces
100ml/3½fl oz/scant ½ cup double
  (heavy) cream
60ml/4 tbsp golden (light corn) syrup
sugar flowers

1 Preheat the oven to 180°C/350°F/ Gas 4. Spray both parts of a 21cm/ 8½in silicone doughnut cake mould with non-stick baking oil, or brush with melted butter.

2 Place the softened butter, caster sugar and vanilla extract in a bowl, and whisk together until light and creamy. Add the eggs, one at a time, whisking to make sure the first one is fully incorporated before adding the second.

3 Sift the flour, baking powder and salt into the mixture, and fold in. Add the milk, and mix just until it all comes together.

4 Divide the batter between the two moulds, spreading evenly, then place in the middle of the oven and bake for 30–35 minutes, or until golden brown. Remove from the oven and leave to stand for 5 minutes before removing the cakes from the moulds. Transfer to a wire rack to cool completely.

5 For the chocolate buttercream, whisk the butter with the icing sugar until crumbly. Beat in the cream, until the buttercream is smooth and thick. Add the cocoa powder, and fold in until smooth and combined.

6 To make the chocolate glaze, melt the chocolate, cream and syrup together in a non-stick pan over a low heat, stirring until smooth and glossy. Remove the pan from the heat and set aside.

7 Take the 'hollow' half of the doughnut cake, and fill the hollow with the chooclate buttercream, spreading it evenly around the hollow. Place the other half of the cake on top, creating a doughnut ring.

8 Cover the cake with the chocolate glaze, pouring it over so that it drizzles down the sides. Top with some sugar flowers, then allow to set before slicing.

Energy 6524kcal/27300kJ; Protein 65.5g; Carbohydrate 770.8g, of which sugars 551.3g; Fat 374.6g, of which saturates 228.3g; Cholesterol 1296mg; Calcium 922mg; Fibre 22.8g; Sodium 2340mg.

Doughnut and butter pudding

I have always been a huge fan of bread and butter pudding, and this one's super easy to make especially if you have any leftover unfilled doughnuts. It is rich, sweet and comforting, and is the ideal dessert to serve on a chilly winter's evening. Serve it with some custard, if you like.

Serves |5–6

5–6 cold cooked unfilled doughnuts
  (use the recipe for Jam-Filled
  Doughnuts on page 28, but do
  not add the filling)
30g/1¼oz/2½ tbsp butter, softened
25g/1oz/⅙ cup raisins
25g/1oz/⅙ cup sultanas
  (golden raisins)
250ml/8fl oz/1 cup full-fat
  (whole) milk
50ml/2fl oz/¼ cup double
  (heavy) cream
2 eggs, beaten
20g/¾oz/1½ tbsp caster
  (superfine) sugar
ground cinnamon, for sprinkling
ground nutmeg, for sprinkling
apricot jam, for brushing
icing (confectioners') sugar,
  for sprinkling

1 Preheat the oven to 180°C/350°F/ Gas 4. Cut the doughnuts into slices and spread both sides of the slices with butter, then arrange in a 23 x 30cm/ 9 x 12in ovenproof dish, overlapping the slices. Sprinkle over the raisins and sultanas.

2 Gently heat the milk and cream together in a pan until hot but not boiling. Remove from the heat. Lightly whisk the eggs with the sugar in a heatproof bowl, and then pour the warm milk mixture over the egg mixture, stirring constantly.

3 Pour this mixture evenly over the doughnut slices and fruit, then sprinkle with cinnamon and nutmeg. Bake in the middle of the oven for 30 minutes, or until golden brown.

4 Brush the top of the pudding with apricot jam while it is still warm, then sprinkle with icing sugar.

COOK'S **TIP**
You can use simple sugar-dusted ring doughnuts (see page 22), but I like using unfilled plain round doughnuts, as they give a good even coverage of the tin.

Energy 398kcal/1661kJ; Protein 7.3g; Carbohydrate 34.9g, of which sugars 19g; Fat 26.4g, of which saturates 11.7g; Cholesterol 124mg; Calcium 109mg; Fibre 0.2g; Sodium 218mg.

Index

This edition is published by Aquamarine
an imprint of Anness Publishing Ltd
108 Great Russell Street, London WC1B 3NA
info@anness.com
www.aquamarinebooks.com; www.annesspublishing.com

If you like the images in this book and would like to investigate using them for publishing, promotions or advertising, please visit our website www.practicalpictures.com for more information.

Publisher: **Joanna Lorenz**
Editor: **Kate Eddison**
Photographer and prop stylist: **Mowie Kay**
Food stylists: **Bruce Martin and Mowie Kay**
Designer: **Lisa Tai**
Production controller: **Mai-Ling Collyer**

Front cover image shows Simple sugar-dusted ring doughnuts (page 22–23), Chocolate-honey glazed ring doughnuts (page 40–41), Oatmeal doughnuts (page 110–11) and Iced eggless ring doughnuts (page 52–53).

The publishers would like to thank the following for permission to reproduce their images: EPA European Pressphoto Agency B.V./Alamy p8; Martí Sans/Alamy p9 (top); Damons Point Light/Alamy p9 (right); David Wei/Alamy p9 (left).

PUBLISHER'S NOTE

NOTES

- Bracketed terms are intended for American readers.
- For all recipes, quantities are given in both metric and imperial measures and, where appropriate, in standard cups and spoons. Follow one set of measures, but not a mixture, because they are not interchangeable.
- Standard spoon and cup measures are level.
  1 tsp = 5ml, 1 tbsp = 15ml, 1 cup = 250ml/8fl oz.
- Australian standard tablespoons are 20ml. Australian readers should use 3 tsp in place of 1 tbsp for measuring small quantities.
- American pints are 16fl oz/2 cups. American readers should use 20fl oz/2.5 cups in place of 1 pint when measuring liquids.
- Electric oven temperatures in this book are for fan ovens. When using a conventional oven, the temperature will probably need to be increased by about 10–20°C/20–40°F. Since ovens vary, you should check with your manufacturer's instruction book for guidance.
- The nutritional analysis given for each recipe is calculated per portion (i.e. serving or item), unless otherwise stated. If the recipe gives a range, such as Serves 4–6, then the nutritional analysis will be for the smaller portion size, i.e. 6 servings. The analysis does not include optional ingredients, such as salt added to taste.
- Medium (US large) eggs are used unless otherwise stated.